D1297442

THE ART AND SKILL OF DELEGATION

THE ART AND SKILL OF DELEGATION

Lawrence L. Steinmetz, Ph.D.
HIGH YIELD MANAGEMENT, INC.

ADDISON-WESLEY PUBLISHING COMPANY
READING, MASSACHUSETTS • MENLO PARK, CALIFORNIA
DON MILLS, ONTARIO • WOKINGHAM, ENGLAND • AMSTERDAM
SYDNEY • SINGAPORE • TOKYO • MADRID • BOGOTÁ
SANTIAGO • SAN JUAN

Sixth Printing, February 1986

 Printed in the United States of America. Published simultaneously in Canada. Library of Congress Catalog Card No. 75-28727.

ISBN 0-201-07269-6
FGHIJKLM-AL-89876

PREFACE

This book is a result of some ten years experience I have had in conducting seminars, executive development programs, and supervisory/management training sessions on the Art and Skill of Delegation. It deals not so much with theory as with practical application.

In those years of working with supervisors, managers, and executives it became obvious to me that the art and skill of delegation is not practiced in the same way at all levels of a given organization or in different organizational structures. The problems of delegation faced by the chief executive of a large corporate or governmental structure are not the same as those faced by the entrepreneur of a small business, or by the manager in the technical laboratory or R & D facility, or by the direct line supervisor of a production line, sales floor, or order department.

Actually, all supervisors delegate. However, the job of delegation at the lower supervisory levels in large organizational structures—what this book refers to as the direct-supervision stage of management—is more a problem of making work assignments than it is true delegation. The direct supervisor gives clear-cut instructions about what is expected to be done, by who, when, and why.

Sometimes, but by no means always, he or she may also include instructions on how to do the work.

The boss of the direct supervisor—what this text refers to as the supervisor of supervisors—delegates differently. He or she is still responsible for getting work done—on the assembly line, on the retail sales floor, in the hospital, or wherever—but by supervising supervisors who, in turn, oversee the work being done and make the direct job assignments. The supervisor of supervisor's job, then, is one of delegating projects to the direct supervisor who, in turn, makes work assignments.

In a relatively small organization—with, say, 15 to 100 people—the problem of the owner/manager/chief cook and bottlewasher/executive is much like that of the supervisor of supervisors. He or she does not directly supervise the "doing" operations but, nevertheless, is under intense pressure to make sure that job assignments are properly made and carried out.

For the manager of managers—the executive of a large corporate structure or governmental agency, and boss of the supervisor of supervisors—the job of delegation is again different. The manager of managers may delegate to a supervisor of supervisors the responsibility for completing an entire project. For example, a chief executive of a large automobile manufacturing plant may well delegate the whole job of design of a new automobile to a subordinate executive, the whole job of developing an advertising campaign to another subordinate, and lobbying in government offices to yet a different subordinate. The point here is that the total job responsibility as a complete function is delegated and the manager of managers is only worried about seeing to it that the whole matrix of organizational responsibilities is performed as it should be done.

Also, problems of delegation for the supervisor in the highly technical laboratory or the staff function differ from those of other supervisors. The personalities, temperaments, and dispositions of employees in these jobs are usually different from those of other personnel. The text explores many of these differences and considers ways in which the supervisor in these areas may become an effective delegator.

Another fundamental point which anyone who would be a good delegator must become aware of is that delegation is complicated by two basic problems: (1) The boss may commit certain basic errors in behavior, attitude, or mechanical functions which cause him or her to be relatively inept at making effective delegations or work assignments. This problem, of course, can be chronic, and it limits the advancement of the individual manager to higher, more responsible positions in the organization—or it limits the growth of the owner/manager's business. The text therefore devotes extensive attention to why bosses fail at delegating. (2) The second problem illustrates the old saying that "You can lead a horse to water but you can't make him drink." There are cases in which subordinates somehow, someway, purposefully or subconsciously, fail to shoulder work which is delegated or assigned to them. Occasionally an employee may simply refuse to do certain kinds of work, but more commonly he or she may have certain mental, physical, or other "hangups" which prevent him or her from shouldering responsibility for the assigned job. Because of the nature of these two problems, each of the four different areas of delegation mentioned above are examined from both standpoints: why the boss fails at delegating and why the subordinate sometimes avoids shouldering responsibility.

It is my sincere desire that this book be a useful, practical tool to individual supervisors, managers, executives, or directors in dispatching their duties as effectively as possible in the area of delegation, no matter what their level in an organization or size of that organization. With this in mind I have tried to make this text as simple and straightforward as possible. The text is designed not only to help the individual in his or her own managerial skills but also to facilitate the in-company training programs and university or publicly sponsored management-education training sessions which are conducted for audiences around the country. The text has been designed to be essentially self teaching, and this content has been tested over the years in the training programs I have conducted in the Art and Skill of Delegation at such institutions as the University of Michigan, University of Colorado, Clemson University, Case/Western Reserve University and many other distinguished institutions of learning, as well as in the many private, in-house training sessions I have conducted for any number of private corporations and governmental agencies in the United States and abroad. There are exercises at the end of each chapter designed to help the student understand the points made in the text and also to facilitate the trainer in helping students and/or trainees understand what they have learned and how to utilize it in their own organizations and companies.

I would like to express my deep appreciation to Dr. Albert W. Schrader of the Division of Management Education at the University of Michigan and to Nathaniel Stewart, who made me heir to this program many years ago when he decided to retire from actively teaching this seminar at that institution. Many of the original ideas for this book were given me by these men, and any person familiar with their fine work will recognize their influence in this text.

I do hope the reader of this book finds it useful and the reading of it productive time well spent.

Boulder, Colorado
February 1976

L.L.S.

CONTENTS

INTRODUCTION

It has been stated that Alexander the Great had a remarkable scheme for delegating authority and assigning responsibility to the people under his command. An enlightened administrator for his time, Alexander commanded his generals to marry the daughters of conquered princes, assuming that the conquered countries would then be governed not only for his purposes but also in accordance with their own needs.

It is probably true that not only would that kind of tactic not create the desired outcome in today's world, but also that one would have a great deal of difficulty implementing it.

Unfortunately, many of the problems which today's managers and executives face are similar to Alexander the Great's. To be sure, they are not commanding great armies, nor are they physically conquering whole nations. However, the problems of the line supervisor in getting production machines running, the problems of the company president in assuring that advertising and marketing policies are implemented, and the problems of the department-store buyer are in some ways all the same. Be they men or women, chief executives or first-level supervisors, all must accomplish a basic task: that of getting results through the people that work for them.

The problem of delegation, which is the total subject of this book, is how to accomplish that particular task.

Chapters 1 through 3 of this book are concerned with the problems generally associated with delegation at any level in a business (or other) organization. Chapters 4 and 5 discuss the problems encountered by supervisors and lower-level managers in the smaller organization or at lower levels in a larger organization. Chapters 6 and 7 address the problem of delegation as it is seen by managers at the middle level in larger organizations, and Chapters 8 and 9 consider the delegation/administration problems faced by top-level executives in giant organizations. Chapter 10 treats one of the special problems of effective delegation—the delegation task in technical, staff, and professional organizations.

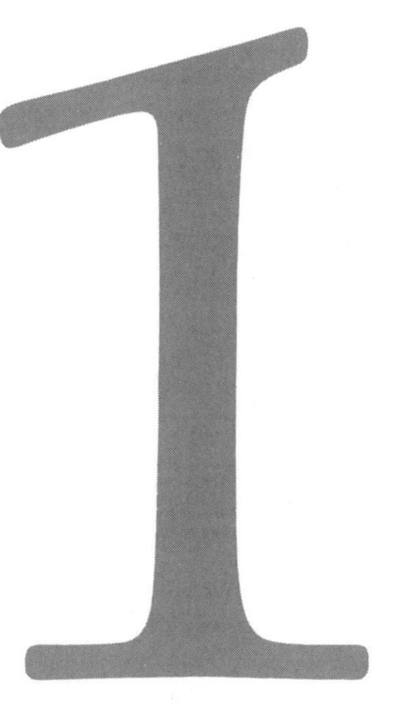

WHAT IS DELEGATION?

In addressing the problem of effective delegation one must answer the basic question—What is delegation? In essence, according to Nathaniel Stewart, effective delegation consists of two things: (1) the farming out of a part of the boss' job domain, and the problems associated therewith, to a subordinate—who also receives the full responsibility to carry that assignment through to its conclusion, making all the necessary decisions along the way; (2) explaining to the delegate the "what" and "why" of a particular problem or job—and leaving the "how" to him or her. In substance, effective delegation frees up executive or supervisory time by enabling subordinates to shoulder the responsibility for the work to be done and decide how it will be accomplished.

There are, of course, some things which delegation is not. Delegation is *not* simply the assignment of work leading to problem identification, with the boss reserving the decision-making prerogatives to himself or herself. Delegation also is not the working on a problem when the decisions which are made are subject to review and discussion by a boss or some participating group. Delegation, in substance, requires the turning over of both the authority and the responsibility for doing a job to a subordinate who is held accountable for the performance of that job.

SOME ELEMENTARY DEFINITIONS

At the outset of any book about delegation the term itself must be defined clearly. The reason for this is that a great deal of confusion —and an enormous amount of erroneous conventional wisdom—is associated with the subject. Even this early in the book the reader undoubtedly has some questions about the use of certain terminology. What, for example, is "authority"? Can one have "authority" without "responsibility," or vice versa? What is meant by "accountability"?

These questions and many more are often bantered about in lecture series, college textbooks, etc., when the subject of effective delegation is discussed. Unfortunately, such pedantic discussions are usually concerned with the development of esoteric terms which belong only in a glossary, and are seldom useful either to the practicing supervisor or the chief executive of the large corporation.

Thus let us define some of these terms right at the outset—but only as to their basic meanings. We will leave the exhausting definitions to the academicians.

Authority—What Is It?

A common lament heard by many management consultants in working with supervisory training groups and executive development programs is: "I could really get things done if I had the authority." Or, "If I was the boss, then I could do it. But my boss won't let me have the authority to get the job done."

Inevitably, the individuals who make these kinds of excuses are the same ones who come out with the jingle which they learned long ago that "Authority must be delegated commensurate with responsibility." Inevitably, the individuals who bemoan the circumstance that they do not have authority to do something are convinced that the reason they don't get results through others is the incompetence of those others—especially their particular boss. They feel that their boss has not followed basic management principles and given them absolute authority to accomplish something. Furthermore, they feel if their boss *had* given them absolute and total authority, everything would be okay.

But just what *is* authority? Is it just the right to fire someone if they don't cooperate? Authority, according to the dictionary, means "legal power"; it also means "one referred to as support for a statement"; and it also means "influence as derived from character, ability, etc." Thus dictionary definitions lead one to believe that "authority" is ambiguous; it can be a legal matter, a citation in a reference work, or a source of influence.

The authority that we are concerned with is actually the third one—a source of influence. Thus, according to our definition, authority is *whatever influence one possesses, at any instant, that will cause someone else to do what the authoritative individual wants that someone to do, at that time.*

Our definition makes it clearly evident that authority can be derived from many sources. Authority can come from physical force—the robber who is waving a gun in front of a victim is quite authoritative. But authority may come from other things—the power of persuasion, for example. Most of us know, either personally or by reputation, at least one person who has been authoritative enough to persuade others to grant him or her various positions of rank, honor, and privilege. And all this because of glibness, not performance.

There are still other sources of authority. The authority of a child who warns the motorist that he or she shouldn't go down a particular road because a bridge is washed out is just as influential as that of the highway patrolman who might tell the same motorist that he or she "will not" attempt to go down that road.

It should be recognized that any supervisor, manager, or executive who has enough authority to cause someone else to do what he or she wants done at that particular moment has all the authority necessary. Yet it should be just as obvious that the source of that authority has many different facets, only one of which is the authority of position. The rest are authorities that are derived from such human factors as knowledge, integrity, and personal attributes of the individual.

For purposes of this book, it is essential that the reader understand what is meant by the line, "You never know how much authority you have until you've exceeded it." That statement might be construed as humorous by some, and indeed it can occasionally lead to an amusing situation, but the truth is that any supervisor, manager, or executive must recognize that they do have the authority to do the things they want to do—*if* they are *capable* of shouldering that authority. For example, it must be recognized clearly that any supervisor should use not only the authority of position, he or she should also use the authority of competence, the authority of personality and the authority of character. Let us look at each of these authority sources and ascertain what they mean for the effective manager or supervisor.

The Authority of Position The authority of position is what most people mean when they refer to "authority." It refers to that title, rank or privilege which gives one person the right to tell another person to do something "or else . . ." The authority of position has real teeth in it. The boss who has the ability to hire and fire certain people has the authority of position over them. Right or wrong, in the authority of position, "the boss is still the boss," as the saying goes.

Unfortunately, the authority of position is the only authority that many insecure managers and supervisors use. They feel that, tyrants though they may be, they must have undying, unwavering obedience to their commands. Such authority, of course, is used every day. Sometimes it is even used by not-otherwise-tyrannical supervisors, managers, and executives. The reason oftentimes is because of a requirement for expediency, health, or safety. An example of this is when an airline pilot (who otherwise is practically always a very amiable individual) gets quite dictatorial in insisting that passengers "Sit down, buckle up, and extinguish cigarettes" because of the anticipation of severe turbulence on a flight.

It should be recognized that the authority of position is a very strong authority source—if one has the position. It also is quite useful. One must necessarily use the authority of position in the proper circumstance. Yet, there are other sources of authority which effective supervisors use. Let us look at them.

The Authority of Competence This authority source depends on one's knowledge or competence. If a person is extraordinarily competent, people will defer authority to that individual. This is especially so if the individual has demonstrated to others that the individual knows what he or she is talking about.

We see the authority of competence clearly demonstrated many times in our workaday lives. Oftentimes a boss will listen to a subordinate when the subordinate says, "We can't do that because . . ." and follows up the "because" with sound reasoning based on the knowledge and experience developed over his or her many years of work experience.

The boss listens to the competent person, just as the patient listens to the doctor. The doctor who tells a patient to avoid certain foods practically always gets cooperation from the patient. The patient cooperates with the doctor not because the doctor has any authority of position over the patient (indeed the doctor actually *works for* the patient) but because he or she accedes to the doctor's knowledge and competence. The doctor who has never been proven wrong or otherwise seen by the patient as unknowledgeable practically always gets better cooperation from a patient than does a doctor who appears incompetent.

The Authority of Personality The authority of personality comes not because its possessor has demonstrated competence or is in a particularly prestigious or authoritative position, but because he or she is easy to work with. Individuals who are easy to talk to, who listen when people talk to them, who are more than willing to work with subordinates, will find that the people with whom they are working will practically always bestow upon them the authority of personality. On the other hand, individuals who are hard to do business with (such as those lovingly referred to as "the south end of a north-bound horse") will have difficulty finding others who will cooperate with them, give them the benefit of the doubt, or otherwise accede to their demands or wishes when they don't otherwise have to.

The authority of personality is sometimes hard for supervisors to recognize, not only as to what it is but how to use it. People who tend to be brusque—and especially people who demand acceptance of the authority of position—don't truly appreciate the authority of personality. Unfortunately, they think other people simply won't work with them. It is too bad that they fail so tremendously in the use of this additional source of authority.

The Authority of Character In a way, the authority of character is derived from one's personal "credit rating" in the eyes of other people. That is, a person's honesty, loyalty, sincerity, reliability, etc., as demonstrated in their past work with other people, determines the amount of respect and obedience they get. People believe that those who have authority of character will do what they say they will do. They will meet production schedules; they will deliver on promises. They do not lie, nor change their story when "the heat is on." They don't try to cheat, nor do they otherwise try to pull "fast ones" in work relationships (or in any other relationship, for that matter).

Individuals who acquire respect from the trail of behavior they leave behind develop the authority of character. Those who acquire disrespect from a behavioral trail of broken promises, unfulfilled expectations, lies, etc., will never have it. No one cares to work with a liar. The reason, of course, is that a liar is unreliable and unpredictable and thus very hard to work with.

All Faces of Authority Work Together Many times people do not realize the power limitations of the various sources of authority available to them. Historical examples can be developed from any walk of life, from any business or organization, to demonstrate that the use of *authority of position* as a sole source of authority is not always effective. For example, in the waning days of the Watergate incidents in national politics, President Nixon was felt to be an ineffectual leader for the nation, notwithstanding the fact that he was, indeed, the *President of the United States of America.* He had the highest position in the land, and in no way could it be denied that he had tremendous authority of position. Yet, in the last days of his administration, because of how the nation perceived his character and personality—and to some degree his competence—he was totally ineffectual as a leader. He himself indicated that prior to his resignation he perceived this ineffectiveness, and that it had a significant influence on his decision to resign.

It must be realized, as we discuss the art and skill of delegation, that all bosses should have sufficient sources of authority available to them to accomplish the goals or objectives they want to accomplish. That is, bosses must be given the authority of position required to do the job, but they can help themselves by developing the *other forms of authority* they need to accomplish the jobs and tasks delegated to them. Competence, after all, can be acquired, personality can be developed, and character and integrity can be cultivated.

Putting the matter of authority to rest, let us address one last fact. *The reason that most bosses do not delegate authority of position to their subordinates is because of the factor of risk involved.* Whenever a boss delegates total authority of position to a subordinate, he or she is taking the risk that the subordinate will use that authority in an unjustifiable, tyrannical manner. When this occurs, problems always develop. Thus many executives, managers (and even line supervisors) are reluctant to delegate the authority of position to subordinates. This is a natural, human trait.

In the same vein, it must be recognized that subordinates who rely *only* on the authority of position to accomplish tasks, goals, or missions may be ineffectual. Any subordinate has additional sources of authority available to him or her if he or she is energetic, intelligent, friendly, and knowledgable.

Responsibility

In delegating a job to a subordinate, just what is delegated? Is it work? Responsibility? Authority?

It has been indicated that authority must necessarily be made available to subordinates and be used by them. Authority can be delegated—at least the authority of position. But responsibility is different. Many writers differ on the point of whether or not one can delegate responsibility. Many people argue that when one makes a person responsible for doing something, he or she is simply making a person responsible for doing something; *not* delegating responsibility. Instead, they argue, the ultimate responsibility is held by the individual who delegates the work to begin with.

Just what is responsibility? Responsibility consists of the obligation to undertake a specific duty or task within the organization. It can be assigned or assumed, but we are concerned here with responsibility that is assigned—that is placed upon a person. When a person is made responsible for getting out a report, putting together a budget, developing a policy, or coming up with a plan, the boss who made that subordinate responsible for that task has, in essence, delegated or assigned the task to the subordinate.

Responsibility therefore comes with the assignment of work to a person. There are limits, of course; a person cannot be held "responsible" for making sure that the sun doesn't shine tomorrow because he or she doesn't have the "authority" to do so. It must be recognized that the notion of authority and responsibility are coextensive.

Suffice it to say that one cannot be given responsibility if they do not have the "authoritative" mechanical abilities to do a job. However, assuming the mechanical, physical, capacity for doing a job, those who have work assigned to them are made responsible for doing it. They therefore are required to use and/or develop sources of authority required to accomplish that job. It is true that a person whose signature is not "authorized" cannot be held responsible for signing checks, but given the fact that his or her signature is authorized (a mechanical problem), then he or she should be able to shoulder the responsibility delegated by his or her boss.

Accountability

"Accountability" is another term oftentimes used in discussing delegation. The purist will often argue that "authority cannot be delegated without responsibility," but that is not the important question. The argument, they say, concerns the question of accountability.

Essentially, accountability consists of assessing what a person did on a particular job. If a person has failed to do a job, he or she has either failed to develop and/or use authority as he or she should have done or has not shouldered the responsibility for accomplishing the job. As management expert Franklin G. Moore has said, "Telling people to do certain things and having them do it are two different things." Sometimes people do what they are asked to and sometimes they don't. Practically always, of course, they have an excuse for not having done what they were supposed to. Sometimes they even have a good reason for failing. But good management principles, particularly those of effective delegation, necessarily hold a person accountable for failing to perform as required, irrespective of the reasons for that failure.

It must be recognized that accountability is essential for good delegation. If people are not held accountable for failing to perform the work delegated to them, all discipline within the organization will be gone. People will do only that which they want to do and will fail to do those things they don't care about.

Many supervisors, managers, and executives fail to make effective delegations because they drop the ball at the point of accountability. They do not realize that accountability is the feedback loop which tells whether the delegated work has (or has not) been done. Obviously, remedial or corrective steps cannot be taken by the manager if he or she does not know that some work has gotten behind, has not been finished, or has been performed at an unacceptable level. One of the principal reasons so many managers fail at making good work assignments and delegating effectively to their subordinates is that they do not use any feedback loop to tell them about the progress of the jobs or projects they have assigned. They have no way of knowing whether or not the work is being accomplished and is coming along on schedule. When that is the case they are very reluctant to delegate, usually preferring to do the job themselves to be sure that it gets done.

ESSENTIALS OF GOOD DELEGATION

The definitional problems outlined above must be dealt with in any book on the subject of delegation if its readers are to gain any insight about improving their delegating skills. To that end we have already indicated that a good delegator must recognize (1) what authority he or she has, (2) what responsibility really means, and (3) the importance of holding someone accountable. However, effective delegation also involves certain other essential factors at the workbench, in the executive suite, or anywhere in between. The nature of delegation changes as one progresses from the shop to the suite, and we will deal with those changes in some detail in Chapter 2. But first we must (1) consider those other essential elements of effective delegation and (2) determine just what is not delegatable.

Having a Feel for the Situation

For good delegation the boss, or whoever assigns work, must have a feel for what the task to be delegated really amounts to. It's very difficult to make effective work assignments when one does not totally understand what the work to be assigned involves. It's easy for an operating supervisor to tell a subordinate to develop a plan for training new employees how to operate a particular machine. But unless that supervisor understands what is involved in learning how to run that machine, difficulties can arise. For example: How much time must be alloted for the assignment? How can it be coordinated with the subordinate's present schedule? Can the plan be completed by the time the supervisor needs it or must the supervisor change his or her own schedule? To demonstrate the importance of knowing what is involved in a given assignment, the reader might consider whether he or she would feel competent to develop a program for training submariners. Of course, if the reader has been trained in the various jobs associated with running a submarine, then he or she *will* feel competent. But note that that competence comes from already having a feel for the situation.

Understanding Existing Policies, Systems, Limitations

A second essential ingredient of good delegation is for the boss to clearly understand any existing policies or procedures governing the task he or she is assigning, as well as of any controlling systems or other limitations which might be placed on the work as it is to be done by the subordinate.

A boss' failure to understand existing policies, systems, or limitations is oftentimes the reason for the lament of subordinates that the boss is not giving them sufficient authority to do a particular job. Without such understanding, the boss will sometimes try to assign a subordinate a task which the subordinate cannot possibly do because of physical, mechanical, or legal limitations. The most personable, competent, and honest individual will not be able to accomplish the delegated task of opening a bank vault legally without the required authority.

Clarification of End Results

Another requirement for effective delegation by any operating supervisor, manager, or executive is that they clarify what end result is expected from the work delegated.

A great deal of attention will be devoted later in this book to the subject of how one clarifies one's performance expectations when work is delegated. However, as for now, the person who is attempting to develop skills in effective delegation should recognize that proper delegation necessarily specifies precisely what performance is expected from the individual who is being made responsible—*and* accountable—for a job.

Accessibility of the Boss

Good delegation also requires that the boss be accessible to the delegatee *after* the work has been delegated. Many supervisors would like to be able to just say, "Fred do this," or "Mary do that," and then forget about the assignment until the work was completed. That's an ideal circumstance, but effective delegation—particularly for complex or involved jobs—cannot be accomplished in that manner. The effective delegator must establish checkpoints and milestones for any assignment so that he or she may have sufficient control to determine that satisfactory progress is being made. For this there must be some communication between the delegatee and the delegator and that means that the boss must be accessible to the subordinate.

One note of caution: While it is true that one must be accessible to his or her subordinates and communicate with them about their work assignments, it is *not* true that one must *always* and *unequivocally* be available to them. The reason for this is that some subordinates—especially those who are insecure—will take advantage of a boss who is *too easily accessible* by continually coming in and asking advice, soliciting opinions, presenting inconsequential or inane problems, occupying the boss's time. Not only does this waste the boss's time, it also wastes that of the subordinate, who could be better spending it by working on his or her delegated task. Furthermore, if the boss actually makes decisions for the subordinate *when the decisional area is within the purview, capability, and talents of the subordinate,* then the subordinate has actually managed to redelegate or reassign the work which he or she was originally given *back to the boss!* Obviously this becomes an intolerable situation, not to mention an expensive time-waster. So the boss's accessibility to subordinates, while necessary, must be regulated by whether or not what is to be communicated *needs* to be communicated.

Establishment of Controls

A good supervisor must establish controls by which to determine what progress is being made on the job he or she has assigned. There is always the possibility of unexpected problems, and sometimes these can be catastrophic if not controlled. It's even possible that either the subordinate or the delegator could be seriously hurt (physically or professionally or both) if certain checks or control systems are not established.

Good delegators have learned over the years that they must

develop control systems for determining the progress made on the tasks, projects, or jobs assigned. This is especially necessary when the work they have delegated has been redelegated to someone else, for then the work is two steps removed from the person whose ultimate responsibility it is. This is a common problem at the executive level in any organization. When the president of a corporaton, for example, asks a vice president of marketing to develop an advertising budget for the forthcoming years, the vice president probably should *not* be the one who develops that budget. Rather, he or she should *re*delegate at least some portions of that responsibility to subordinates who are responsible for actually allocating particular segments of the advertising budget. To illustrate: to the subordinate manager in charge of the firm's soft goods would be redelegated the job of developing an advertising budget for those soft goods; while another individual would be redelegated the advertising budget for hard goods.

Necessarily, the president of the company is going to hold the vice president of marketing responsible for developing the budget, as well as for any mistakes that may occur in it. Yet the president should be aware of the fact that it is not that vice president's function to build budgets himself or herself (unless ordered to do so by the president); rather it is to have the budget developed by those people who are most familiar with its various aspects—and to review the budget before forwarding it to the president.

In this redelegation process the president is necessarily running a risk that the vice president of marketing will fail—and also that the managers of soft goods and hard goods will fail. In order to avoid these potential problems it is common for good executives to establish control methods to ensure that various portions of the job which have been redelegated are "coming along." This does *not* mean that the president checks personally with the soft goods and hard goods managers—to do so would be considered meddling, and would be extremely poor form. Instead, the president would ask for progress reports from the vice president to ensure that things are progressing as desired. It is then incumbent on the vice president to know when things are *not* on target and to take corrective or remedial action. If such action is not effective, then the vice president must bring this fact to the attention of the president.

Preparedness of the Delegatee

Work cannot be effectively delegated unless the delegatee is prepared to handle it. This means that the delegatee must have acquired the training and experience needed to enable him or her to perform the task for which he or she will be held accountable. However, a note of caution on this point: Many people will use the excuse that they are not ready to undertake a specific task because they have not had sufficient *experience.* But it must be recognized that experience must be obtained for the first time in *any* person's life. Every airline pilot must solo for the first time; every neurosurgeon must plunge a blade into the living brain for the first time. In each such case the person performing the action has no *experience* for it—but they do have the *training* for it.

Many supervisors speak of lack of *experience* when they mean lack of *training.* But that is incorrect. Certainly a person who has not had sufficient training for it cannot be expected to perform a particular job. However, if a person has had sufficient training but not "sufficient experience," there is no reason to withhold the assignment from him or her. In fact, if the subordinate is properly trained to do the job, this is the time to give him or her the opportunity to get the experience.

Awareness and Recognition of Risk

The last requirement we shall mention for the effective delegation of work is this: Every boss must clearly recognize that there is always some risk that the job assigned will not get done. Problems can arise which could prevent the completion of the task, and the boss must not only recognize them but also warn the delegatee of them. One cannot realistically delegate or assign work to someone when they're unaware of the risk involved, especially if the subordinate is also unaware of the risk. Certainly the latter cannot be held accountable for the successful completion of a work assignment if the boss knew of potential risks but didn't bother to warn the subordinate of them.

Later on in the book we will discuss in some detail the necessity for the boss to be able to recognize and tolerate risk and uncertainty if he or she is to be an effective delegator of work. For now, suffice it to say that every work assignment involves risk, and the boss who is unaware of it, does not accept it, or fails to inform the subordinate of it will never be effective in making job assignments.

WHAT IS NOT DELEGATABLE

Many bosses fail at assigning work to subordinates because they really don't know what they should and should not delegate. Some think that the way to delegate is to simply assign all the work one can to one's subordinates, find out what those subordinates *can't* do, and do that part of the job oneself. This is not true delegation.

Intelligent managers who are adept at the art and skill of delegation have very definite ideas about what they can and cannot delegate. While what is delegatable varies between levels of management in any organization, there are some basic nondelegatable tasks common to all levels—tasks at which the subordinate would almost surely fail. We will discuss these tasks in the remainder of this chapter.

Conceptual Planning

Conceptual planning is generally not delegatable, particularly when it is an integral part of a larger plan or objective. It is possible for a boss to delegate to a subordinate the job of planning a campaign or a strategy, or developing a policy or implementing a scheme. However, one cannot delegate a planning task when it is a conceptual part of a master plan. Inevitably, unless the individual who plans part of an overall or master plan is given very clear directions or limits beforehand, he or she will be incapable of coming up with a scheme which is *compatible* with the total plan. Thus, planning, at least from a conceptual stance, must be done by the boss who (presumably) sees the total output to be required as a result of the plan.

Morale Problems

Bosses also cannot delegate problems associated with morale—particularly if they are significant problems for the totality of the boss's work unit. Just as it would be imprudent for the president of a company to ask his or her secretary to stand in for the president at the company's annual awards banquet, so would it be improper for the line supervisor to have someone else give his or her immediate subordinate a pat on the back (or other form of recognition) for that supervisor. Sometimes a substitute is simply not acceptable, and when that is the case, delegation of the task is inappropriate.

Reconciling Differences Between Separate Organizational Units

Another area of managerial responsibility which usually is not delegatable is the reconciliation of differences between separate, identifiable units under the boss's control. A classic example of this is the conflicts which arise between line and staff members in a business. Inevitably the line is more concerned with production and making a profit, while the staff is concerned with less tangible—yet still very real factors—such as morale. When differences arise between what the line wants to do and what the staff wants to do it is very difficult for an executive officer to delegate to a subordinate the reconciliation of these differences, particularly if that subordinate happens to be a member of the line group or the staff group. Inevitably the guiding hand of the senior executive is required.

Coaching and Developing Direct Subordinates

Coaching or personal development activities which the boss conducts with an immediate subordinate usually cannot be delegated. This is not to say that a line supervisor cannot delegate to the training department the requirement of teaching one of his or her subordinates how to operate a machine. The point is that when there is an official and personal relationship between the supervisor and the subordinate as to where the subordinate is to grow and develop in shouldering additional responsibility, this coaching must necessarily be done on a one-to-one basis between the boss and the subordinate. It cannot be delegated to other people within the organization.

Reviewing the Performance of Subordinate

It seems pretty obvious that the appraisal or review of one's immediate subordinate's performance is another task which cannot be delegated to someone else in the organization. About the only exception to this case might be when one's immediate subordinate has been on loan to some other department or organization and *has actually been working for a different supervisor or boss.* Barring that situation, the boss of the immediate subordinate is the only person who should be qualified to make any true assessment of the merits of the individual's performance. Furthermore, for purposes of morale it would be insufferable to violate the idea that one's immediate superior should assess one's performance.

Any Direct Assignment That Has Been Given to You, Specifically

On occasion bosses have reasons for requiring a particular subordinate to do a particular job. Whenever *your* boss has specified that *you,* and no one else, will do a particular job, then that task is generally not delegatable.

Usually, of course, when subordinates are told to do something, it is fully expected that they, in turn, will redelegate or reassign those tasks to yet other subordinates within the operation. This is a normal circumstance when chief executives delegate work to subordinate managers who, in turn, delegate or reassign work to line supervisors. However, for reasons of training, development, or confidentiality, bosses sometimes consider it advisable that a particular subordinate perform a specific task. And in such a case it would be imprudent for that subordinate to give the job to someone else.

Confidential Work

Another area of managerial responsibility that cannot be delegated is work which is confidential in nature—especially if there are no subordinates who have the requisite security clearance. Usually the term "security clearance" makes one think of government work, national security, and intrigue. However, many business organizations require that their employees treat information about products, designs, processes, or whatever as confidential. For example, an attorney's secretary must not be a talker; not everyone in an office should know the combination of the office safe; and a couturiere's new designs are treated as top secret.

Examples of the need for confidentiality within business organizations are ubiquitous. Many young, naive, or inexperienced people do not truly appreciate this need. Almost any business has, at some stage, information or knowledge which must be processed yet controlled if the business is to function as it should. Consequently, supervisors dealing with confidential matters must recognize that they cannot delegate things which would in any way compromise confidential material.

Only Part of a Problem

Parts of problems (as opposed to whole problems) cannot normally be delegated. This is not an ironclad rule; a part of a problem can sometimes be delegated if what is needed for its solution can be clearly defined.

However, if someone is working on the *whole* problem (or on a solution involving that part of the problem one wants to delegate) it would be foolhardy to delegate a portion of the problem to someone else. For example, it would be ridiculous for a manufacturer of slide projectors to ask one employee to find and fix the fault that causes slides to hang up—while at the same time asking someone else to redesign the mechanism so the slides will move faster. Either employee, in solving his or her own problem, might solve the other's problem as well (or make it much more difficult, for that matter).

Pet Projects

Beware of pet projects. It's one thing for a manager to be conducting a pet project "on the side" in search of new ideas or knowledge relevant to the company's business. It is entirely something else if the project is *not* so related. In the first instance, delegation of the activity to a subordinate may or may not be acceptable to the organization—a matter which should be determined beforehand. In the second instance, there's no question about it—it's wrong. Not only will it breed resentment and lower morale, it may also be illegal. Perhaps the most common illustration of illegal delegation is that of the executive who asks a secretary to do some personal shopping for him or her on company time. This practice is widely done and frequently winked at, but consider how it could be interpreted: Since the secretary is being paid by the company while doing personal errands for the boss, the boss is technically diverting company funds to personal use. That might be just enough of a lever to cost an unpopular boss his or her job. Also, such personal service might be considered indirect income, and so be taxable. In general, then, pet projects are not delegatable.

EXERCISES

1. Does delegation of authority imply that a person has responsibility for doing a job?
2. What are the "four sources of authority"? Do they exist in your organization? What are some examples of each source as it exists in your organization?
3. Is there any way one can determine how much authority he or she has in your organization without exceeding it? How?
4. Give some examples of situations in which you didn't feel you had been delegated sufficient authority of position to adequately do your job.
5. How is one held accountable for projects delegated to him or her in your organization? Could this be improved? How?
6. In your company or organization, which is more necessary for effective delegation to exist—being readily accessible to ones' subordinates or taking the chance that the subordinate may fail? Give examples.
7. Why do we say that planning may not be a delegatable task? Do you agree? Why or why not?

CHANGING PATTERNS OF DELEGATION

The serious student of the art and skill of delegation will recognize that there are changing dimensions in the practice of delegation, largely because the nature of the work which is being supervised, managed, or administered differs within different levels of an organization. As the nature and complexity of the work require more independence of action on the part of the subordinate, and especially as the amount and quantity of the required intellectual activity increases, the nature of the delegation task begins to change.

The change process is, at the outset, very dramatic, but at the higher levels becomes quite subtle. The reason for this is that as an individual grows professionally, he or she becomes more capable of adjusting to the new strategems and tactics that are required at his or her new level of (increased) responsibility in the organization. Then, too, it must be recognized that at the higher levels in organizations people are usually "groomed" for their jobs, oftentimes having been put in training positions and usually having been helped via coaching and other developmental activities. Similar preparation is not often done at lower levels, although it should be.

DELEGATION FOR THE FIRST-LEVEL SUPERVISOR

Once an individual has been promoted to first-level supervisor, he or she presumably is in line to eventually become a manager. However, at least in most larger organizations, the first-level (or direct) supervisor's activities and functions are still very tightly controlled by his or her own supervisor. The direct supervisor almost always oversees very mechanical activities. If he or she is bossing an assembly line facility, the work load is very clearly spelled out, the line is practically always machine paced, and poor quality work is inevitably pinpointed by quality control or quality assurance people. About all the line supervisor has to worry about is getting his or her people to do a job that is fairly clearly defined. Very little profound thought is expected of the line supervisors, and true flexibility in terms of designating who is to do what, when, and under what circumstances (the preliminaries for effective delegation) is not really a requirement.

The same thing is true if the line supervisor is supervising nonproduction line activities. The assistant manager in the department store, overseeing store clerks, is still supervising a fairly mechanistic function. His or her employees wait on customers, write up sales, assist customers in the selection of merchandise, and sell products. But what they do and what they have to work with is still fairly tightly controlled.

In the same manner people in other activities at the lower supervision levels are fairly tightly regimented. The office manager in a stenography pool really only tells people what to do and when and where to do it, checks up to see that it was done, and takes corrective action if it wasn't. Just so with the head teller in a bank, or the foreman on a construction crew. In all cases plans are being followed in a rather rigid, mechanistic fashion. The direct supervisor may be equipped—and destined—for higher positions, but first-line supervision has little flexibility in terms of what is to be done, or when or how it is to be done.

DELEGATION FOR THE HIGHER-LEVEL MANAGER —OR ULTIMATELY, THE EXECUTIVE

When an individual advances beyond first-level supervisor the dimensions of the work which he or she is overseeing begin to change—yet the individual often receives little help in adapting to this change. As a supervisor of supervisors the individual is no longer directly overseeing the "doing" aspects of the job. Rather he or she is in the position of coordinating the activity of several "doing" functions within the organization. (See Fig. 1)

In the middle levels of management (what we will refer to as the "supervisor-of-supervisors stage") the individual oversees the activities of line supervisors. They, in turn, are responsible for seeing that the mechanistic functions are accomplished by the rank and file at the "doing" level in the organization. Something very dramatic occurs when an individual is promoted to this position. He or she is no longer restricted by the mechanical nature of the first-level supervisor's job, but becomes more of a planner, problem-solver, and schedule-meeter. Practically always at this organizational level one can assume that he or she can deal with the problems that occur at work by exercising leadership qualities, but that

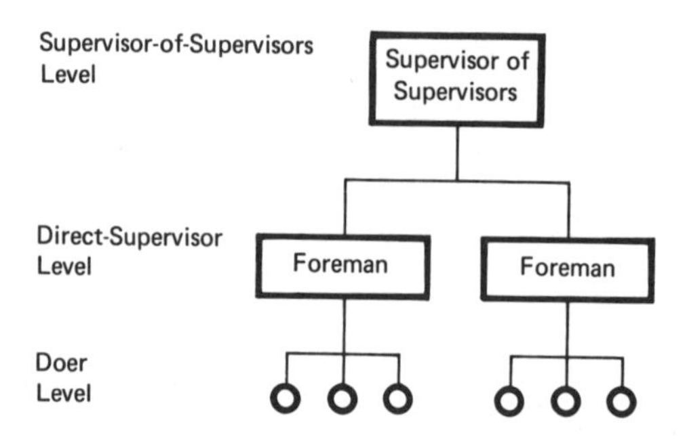

Figure 1

someone else will actually *do* the work. Thus the nature of the supervision required at this position is of a secondary level rather than primary.

Necessarily, when things go wrong on the work floor it is the line supervisor's responsibility to remedy the situation. However, the line supervisors are not always able to do this. For example, a line supervisor seldom is capable of overriding decisions made by higher management—and if higher management's decision not to purchase something at the end of the fiscal period creates a raw material shortage for a production unit, the line supervisor will be faced with a problem over which he or she has little or no control. So these kinds of problems are bumped up to the supervisor of supervisors for resolution.

The supervisor of supervisors will assess these problems in a different vein than will the line supervisor. Inevitably it is not *only* a question of one unit being "down" because of material shortage; other problems always enter in. Then the questions broaden and become more important: How does one meet production or delivery schedules; how does one resolve QC problems in tooling, etc.? Now the supervisor of supervisors must truly begin to manage. He or she must plan, organize, direct, and control the activities not only of the rank and file but also of those who supervise the rank and file of that and other departments.

At the supervisor-of-supervisors stage it is imperative that the manager have knowledge and understanding of a rather broad array of work activities. No longer will the "Let's roll up our sleeves and get after it" routine save the day. The supervisor of supervisors is only one person trying to get results from many people and machines. He or she must thoroughly understand the overall goals and objectives of the unit with which he or she is concerned, whether that unit deals with production, records, marketing, quality assurance, finance, personnel, or industrial relations. At the supervisor-of-supervisor's level vision and perspective are required. Now the boss must actually *manage* by integrative effort, rather than by prodding production or job performance via continual pressure or constant surveillance.

On to the Executive Suite

The problems of the supervisors of supervisors are very similar to the problems of top-level executives in an organization. However, there is a definite difference between the activities required of the true executive and those required of the supervisor of supervisors.

For our purposes we will define the executive level in an organization as the management-of-managers level, as distinct from the supervisor-of-supervisors level and the direct-supervisor level which we talked about previously. At the top-executive, or management-of-managers, level the individual responsible for running a major section of a large organization becomes a manager or administrator in the truest sense of the word. At this position the manager actually manages people who, in turn, manage supervisors who, in turn, supervise workers or rank-and-file individuals. This relationship is shown in Fig. 2.

The manager of managers' phase of business is truly different from that of the supervisor of supervisors or a line supervisor. The manager of managers is required to run the total operation. In a small business this would mean that he or she is responsible for everything—marketing plans, development of financial structure, purchase decisions, personnel policies, etc.

In a large organization, however, one becomes a manager of managers without having total control over the entire operation. An executive with a large public utility, for example, may be in charge of a particular geographic subdivision, community, or other municipal unit such as a county, but still be a long way from the

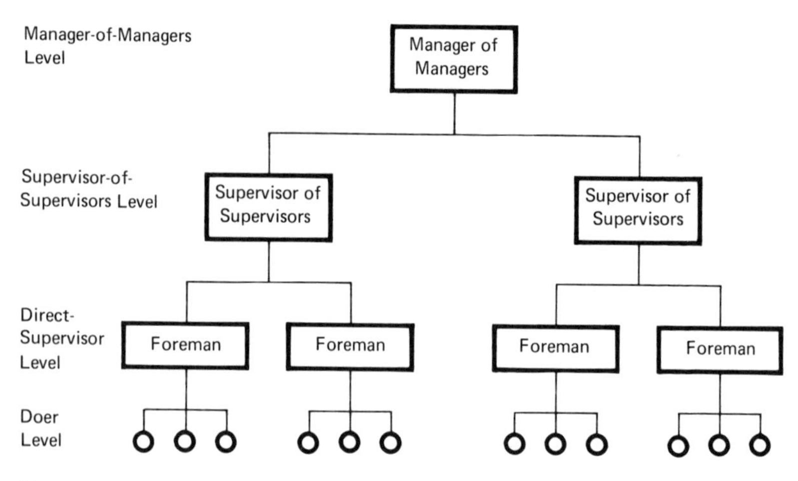

Figure 2

presidency of the corporation. In that capacity, however, that manager is still, truly, a manager of managers. He or she approves budgets, assents to plans for improving the company's image in the community, agrees to construction or distribution plans, accepts operating budgets, and otherwise ratifies or endorses operational decisions which are put together by his or her subordinates. In this capacity the manager of managers is not a doer in any sense of the word. Each subordinate supervisor of supervisors has (theoretically, at any rate) been asked to develop the operating plans, budgets, schedules, and goals they see as being necessary at their level in the organization. They, in turn, develop these items from information received from their direct supervisors.

The manager of managers, therefore, oftentimes is in an approval posture. He or she does little or no mechanical work such as collecting data, putting together operating decisions, scheduling work flow, buying merchandise for resale, etc. His or her problem (and functional obligation within the organization) is to conceptually plan the total direction and thrust for the operating organization or unit. In a large organization these plans, of course, may in turn be approved by yet higher levels of management. In our example the manager of managers in the large public utility may well find that his or her operating plans—which are to be submitted to the president of the corporation—must be integrated with the operating plans of the managers of managers in other areas serviced by that utility. However, at the management-of-managers level there is true flexibility and opportunity for the executive to determine many facets of his or her operating organization. For example, within the constraints established by corporate officers, the manager of managers may be free to reallocate and redistribute operating revenues as he or she sees fit.

THE IMPORTANCE OF THE CHANGING PATTERNS OF DELEGATION

It should be obvious by now that the level one is at in an organization largely determines how his or her work activities can be conducted. Obviously the rank-and-filer must *do* things—run a machine, wait on customers, repair vehicles, or whatever.

The doer's activities are very tightly controlled. But an individual who becomes a supervisor has more flexibility and latitude; he or she can rely more on independent thought and activity. Likewise, when one becomes a supervisor or a manager of managers additional changes occur, changes that require different talents at the art and skill of delegation. For the remainder of this chapter we will discuss some of these major problems and the nature of delegation as it applies to the direct supervisor, the supervisor of supervisors, and the manager of managers.

DELEGATION IN THE SMALL UNIT

In the small unit—a unit supervised by a direct supervisor—delegation activity is limited. In a dictionary sense, delegation means to commit powers and functions to someone else. While it is true that the direct supervisor does commit power and functions to subordinates, such power and functions are fairly rigidly and mechanistically controlled, as we have mentioned. Because of the mechanistic nature of work which is assigned in the small unit, it is best that the operating supervisor understand that his or her function as a delegator is that of making effective work assignments.

Work Assignment vs. Delegation

The intelligent supervisor will not differentiate in his or her mind between making work assignments and the function of delegation. Rather, he or she will simply think of such activity as delegation— even though it may really be direct work assignment.

Making effective work assignments depends on knowing how to tell a person what to do and being sure that they understand it clearly in terms of performance objectives. Management expert James M. Black refers to this as the application of the newspaper formula: "who, what, when, where, how, and why," and we will examine each of these information requirements more closely.

Who In making effective work assignments, the line supervisor must first determine *who* is going to do a particular job. At this level that may not be difficult at all. The direct supervisor may have only one or two or three people working for him or her, and in that case it is simply a question of "who is up next." It should be recognized however, that in assigning the work to the right subordinate, matters of equity, favoritism and other questions will arise. Inevitably, even in the small work unit, someone will feel, "It's not my turn," or (conversely) "Hey, I should have gotten that." Supervisors who are going to be effective at making work assignments and getting work done must be aware of any petty or personal problems that may crop up.

Another important factor is the question of who *really* will be responsible for doing a job in which two or more people are involved. At this stage, anyone making direct work assignments must confront the question of the delegation of authority, responsibility, and accountability as defined in Chapter 1. If two or more individuals are to work on the same job, one of them must be made directly responsible for seeing it through to completion. And that one must also have the authority to oversee the activity. This includes not only authority of position, but also the other three sources of authority discussed earlier. It must also be made clear to the responsible individual that he or she will also be held *accountable* for the proper completion of the activity. Thus, even though the assignment of work at the direct-supervision level may seem like a simple task, it must meet the same conditions required of true delegation at any other level.

What Making effective work assignments also requires that the supervisor define *what* is being assigned to the subordinate. At the direct-supervision level this means defining job performance in terms of quantity, quality, scheduling, time usage, budget constraints, etc. Giving useful job instructions also requires that the supervisor communicate to the subordinate in language that the subordinate understands. But even that may not be sufficient, since misunderstandings do occur. Therefore, it is important that the supervisor double-check to see that the subordinate understands clearly what is expected.

When Effective work assignment also requires that the supervisor specify *when* the individual responsible for the job is expected to perform. Smart supervisors invariably set time limits on the jobs they assign whether or not time is "of the essence." The reason for this is that if there is no deadline, the subordinate can assume that the job is unimportant, that it can just be pushed to the bottom of the pile forever. So to get results—which he or she must always do—the good supervisor sets a time limit on every assignment, whether or not the job is urgent. The deadline may be tight or it may be liberal, but it is always necessary.

Where Though it may seem a bit obvious, it is always well to specify just *where* a job is to be done, as well as where tools, materials, and other essentials for the job may be obtained. When the worker has his or her own workbench and machine, this is simple. But when the worker must go—perhaps in a vehicle—to a distant point to do the job, specifying where can be complex.

How At the direct-supervision level, effective work assignment also requires that the employee be told *how* to do the job. Note that we specify that this is necessary at the *direct-supervision* level. Successful delegation at *higher* levels in the organization does *not* require the manager to tell the subordinate *how* to do the job. In fact, many motivational studies indicate that, at the higher levels of management in any organization, for a boss to tell a subordinate *how* to do a job may seriously demoralize that subordinate.

Many motivational-theory idealists will argue that this will also be true when one tells a rank-and-filer how to do a job. However, recent studies of leadership effectiveness in supervisory capabilities tend to refute this assumption. Many psychologists will argue that the rank and file do *not* especially mind being told how to do a job; indeed, *in certain circumstances,* they *expect* to be told.*

Thus, where delegation is concerned, one important differentiation must be made between the job of the direct supervisor and those of the supervisor of supervisors and the manager of managers. Telling a subordinate how to do a job (at least within certain parameters of end results expected) is extremely important at the direct-supervision level. But it is just as important that the supervisor of supervisors and the manager of managers allow their subordinates a great deal of latitude in determining *how* a job is to be accomplished.

Why There is no argument here with the words of the wise old philosopher: "Always tell your people *why* you are telling them to do something." This is valid at *all* supervisory levels. There's no question but that people are more willing to do things when they know *why* these things need to be done. When they don't clearly understand the necessity, particularly if the task is burdensome, they will often postpone the job or otherwise avoid the responsibility of accomplishing it. Therefore, every supervisor, at every level, should spend whatever time and effort are necessary to explain the need for a particular job to the subordinate to whom it is delegated.

Problems of Making Work Assignments at the Direct-Supervision Level

Lack of cooperation when job assignments are made at direct-supervision levels can be attributed to various reasons, some of which are discussed in the following paragraphs.

---

* Lawrence L. Steinmetz and Charles D. Greenidge, "Realities That Shape Managerial Style," *Business Horizons* (October 1970), **13,** no. 5, pp. 23–32.

Insubordination Occasionally an employee may refuse an assignment out of sheer insubordination. This is not a common occurrence, but when it does happen, the direct supervisor's response is usually determined by union or company regulations.

Opinion Sometimes a subordinate may refuse to accept a job in the belief that it is not within his or her area of responsibility. This most often occurs in union circumstances, where the employee may feel, without intending to be insubordinate, that certain rules or language in the labor contract forbid him or her from performing the task. It may be just that the opinions of the supervisor and the subordinate disagree on interpretation of the rules, or it may be a simple misunderstanding. Sometimes it can be ironed out on the spot; other times it may require a ruling by an arbitrator.

Communication This is a major problem in making work assignments, as it is in all human relationships. The supervisor may not have the knack of giving good instructions, failing to express his or her thoughts clearly or perhaps just not being thorough enough. On the other hand, it may be that the subordinate had his or her mind on other things when the job instructions were given and just failed to pay attention.

Control This, of course, is one of the functions of management. The supervisor *must* check up. He or she has to be sure that: the subordinate has understood the assignment and instructions; the work is being done properly; materials and equipment are available when and where they are needed; the work is progressing on schedule; and so on. Should the supervisor fail to check up as necessary, the job will almost inevitably fall behind, and that would indicate that the supervisor was not performing as he or she should.

Planning Many direct supervisors fail at making really effective assignments because they look not at the whole job but at its pieces. Thus they assign parts of the job, rather than the total responsibility. This results in splintered work assignments, the effect of which is practically always undesirable job performance.

Training One of the responsibilities for any level of management is to ensure that employees are adequately trained to handle the job assignments given them. Many supervisors do an excellent job of training, but oftentimes it can be seen that many employees are ill-prepared to do the work assigned to them. In such cases the supervisor has neglected his or her training responsibility. This does not mean that it is the supervisor's responsibility to train all of his or her employees—that may fall within the purview of the organization's training department. But, it *is* the responsibility of the supervisor to ensure that all of his or her employees *have been* adequately trained to do the jobs that are going to be assigned to them.

By now it should be apparent that making effective work assignments at lower levels in organizations involves many problems. These problems are not unlike those found at higher levels in the organization except that the work being delegated at the lower level is more mechanistic in nature.

Furthermore, the nature of the person to whom the work is delegated is also different. Workers in the rank and file are not usually motivated by the same aspirations and ambitions as are those in higher levels of management. Some people are very ambitious and apparently cannot be given enough work, perhaps even shoulder too much responsibility. But these people are more commonly found at higher levels in the organization. Real eagerness at the "doing" level is most likely to appear only in those who have just started working for the organization. They are usually younger people, perhaps just out of school. Other people in the rank and file are unlikely to be interested in advancement. Some of them simply prefer to do a good job and earn their money, and others would just rather put in an average day's work for a day's pay, but neither wants the responsibilities of a higher position. And then there are those who are interested only in doing as little work as possible for as much money as they can get; obviously they do not seek additional responsibility. Given these circumstances, it is not too surprising that some managers see nothing wrong in having the direct supervisor prod, cajole, or otherwise coerce the rank-and-file workers to perform as he or she thinks they should.

DELEGATION AT THE MIDDLE-MANAGEMENT LEVEL

True delegation must begin to appear at the supervisor-of-supervisors level if the manager is to be effective in running his or her (now larger) operation. At this point, planning and coordination of the activities of subordinate supervisors becomes imperative for success. Responsibility for the accomplishment of work must be delegated, along with commensurate authority, of course. Furthermore, accountability—and the nature of that accountability—must be clearly defined. In addition, because of the changing nature of the problems attendant to effective functioning at this organizational level, it is necessary also that subordinates be given greater freedom to determine *how* they are going to accomplish their jobs. At this stage, the supervisor of supervisors is moving into the true management realm within the organization and can no longer rely on "scream and scare 'em" tactics of management.

Delegation vs. Abdication

Regarding effective delegation, one of the truly common problems found at the supervisor-of-supervisors level in any organization is the problem of abdication. Managerial analysts note that supervisors of supervisors, particularly those new to the job, often abdicate their responsibilities in the matter of job delegation or the making of work assignments. That is, they tend to simply dump jobs on their subordinate supervisors and then hold them accountable for the subsequent performance on those jobs, whether good or bad, while giving them little or no guidance. Their reasoning seems to be that those subordinate supervisors are "grownup men and women" and "should be responsible persons." They assume that those subordinates should understand that when they're told to do something, it is expected to be done, and that is that. Such reasoning, of course, does not inspire a cooperative attitude from the subordinate supervisors.

Supervisors of supervisors must remember that although their subordinates are supervisors too—accustomed to overseeing the activities of the rank and file, practically always conscientious, quick to shoulder responsibility, aggressive, hard working, and willing to take on whatever their boss assigns—this does *not* mean they are automatically capable of assuming responsibility for complex assignments with no direction. Often they may not understand what is actually being asked of them. Sometimes they may not totally integrate those jobs which are given them into the overall scheme of the operation. Because of these factors, the supervisor of supervisors who dumps work on subordinates with no direction, expects them to perform, and expects to hold them accountable for satisfactory job performance, can also expect trouble of some sort—not because the subordinate may not shoulder the responsibility, but because the subordinate does not see or understand the overall plan or operation.

Supervisors of supervisors must realize that effective delegation at their level in the organization requires that they carefully and completely instruct any direct supervisor about what is going to be done, when, by whom, etc. In this respect, the basic ground rules for effective delegation by supervisors of supervisors are very similar to those for direct supervisors. However, since supervisors of supervisors usually deal with ideas and conceptual patterns as much as with mechanistic functions, it is good practice for them to have a mental checklist for some of the essentials of effectively delegated work. There are essentially three primary tests for determining whether a supervisor of supervisors has actually been delegating work or has been abdicating or otherwise abusing his or her responsibility concerning work which should have been delegated. They are as follows:

1. If the work being done by the subordinate is (and has been) of good caliber, probably the supervisor of supervisors is doing a good job of delegation. High-quality work being performed by a subordinate necessarily reflects upon his or her supervisor. Subordinates can seldom do high-quality work if their boss has not been effective at clearly describing to the subordinate what is expected to be done, when, and under what circumstances.

2. Must the supervisor of supervisors make decisions or can the subordinate do that? When work has been effectively delegated, the subordinate has shouldered the responsibility for determining what needs to be done, what would be appropriate action, what solutions might prevail. Supervisors of supervisors who have dele-

gated work effectively practically always find themselves in a position of *approving* those plans or actions decided on by their subordinates.

3. Has the delegation of the job saved the boss' time and released him or her for other important responsibilities? To the uninitiated, assigning job responsibility by simply dumping it on a subordinate will have the desired affect of freeing up time for the supervisor of supervisors. However, experience will show that when one delegates work by abdicating his or her supervisory role, either of two things may happen: (a) The work simply does not get done, or (b) it gets done wrong. Either way, the supervisor of supervisors, whose time should be going into other things, will have to spend time to (a) do what was not done, or (b) straighten out what was done wrong. Effective delegation, at whatever supervisory level, should free the delegator's time for other things.

Indications of Good Delegation

To anyone concerned with the supervisor-of-supervisors level in an organization, and the delegation problems at that level, it should be obvious that good delegation at the middle levels of management requires, above all else, clear-cut definition of any jobs assigned to subordinates. There are several indications of whether or not the supervisor of supervisors has effectively delegated work to his or her subordinates. For example, delegation is effective when:

- ☐ The problems, goals, and expectations for the end product or result are clearly and obviously understood by the subordinate.
- ☐ Controls are set and properly exercised by the superior and, for the most part, allow subordinates sufficient freedom to handle the task their own way, while being responsible for the end result.
- ☐ The individual has the degree of authority (in terms of authority of position) appropriate for the kind of responsibility involved in the delegated task.
- ☐ The delegated task provides a good training experience for the subordinate, allowing him or her to assume responsibility,

make the necessary decisions, and come up with a completed work assignment.

☐ On the whole, the completion of the delegated task contributes to the company's operating effectiveness and accomplishment of organizational goals.

Any supervisor of supervisors who is effective at making delegation work should be able to check off all these indicators for each work assignment he or she makes. If not, this would indicate that he or she has not fully accepted or thoroughly understood what is required for effective delegation at the supervisor-of-supervisors level.

DELEGATION AT THE TOP OF THE LARGE ORGANIZATION

Delegation at the top of any large organization necessarily assumes a posture of true administration. What is required for effective delegation at this level is an attitude of decentralization; that is, the willingness to give subordinates the responsibility (and requisite authority) to accomplish certain functions in the organization.

Everyone knows that decentralization is supposed to reduce cost. Decentralizing the authority and responsibility for a particular job is also supposed to save time, cut paperwork and avoid unnecessary reviews of work done by others. If successful, decentralization should free up executives to do executive work—a true bargain for the company. Any good executive can tell you that his or her assistants, secretaries, and subordinate executives are hired to think, to make important decisions, and to plan ahead for the operation of the organization. Further, most realize that failure to rely upon the talents of one's immediate subordinates will cause the executive to clutter up his or her desk (and mind) with matters that could be handled by others.

It should be recognized that all too often executives who know these things still permit their desks and minds to become cluttered with details. It is not at all uncommon to see presidents and chief executive officers in large organizations opening their own mail, digging materials out of file cabinets, making telephone inquiries, etc. Many times executives do this because they feel it is essential to their successful performance on the job. Unfortunately, time spent on these activities is time lost from the jobs they are actually paid to do.

Being a Manager of Managers

Being a manager of managers is not easy. This is especially true with respect to delegation. Delegation is an art as much as a science, and plying any fine art requires more than the implementation of a set of rules for doing specific things, such as stating policies, defining jobs, or establishing controls. The art of delegation, especially at the management-of-managers level, requires initiative, imagination, self-discipline, and loyalty from people if the executive is to be successful. According to one authority, for a manager of managers to be effective as a delegator, he or she must demonstrate the following four important qualities:

1. *Receptivity.* The manager of managers must be receptive to, and give credit for, other people's ideas. He or she must be willing to recognize that other people (a) do come up with good ideas, (b) can determine how to do jobs as well and effectively as anyone else, and (c) are responsible individuals in their own rights.

2. *Placidity.* The executive must be sufficiently placid in disposition to permit others to make mistakes (albeit mistakes which are not disastrous to the performance of the job or the financial stability of the organization). Making mistakes is something that everybody does. The executive who is unwilling to permit subordinates to make mistakes and learn from them—who fails to view the cost of those mistakes as an investment in the development of the organization's people resources—does not have the disposition required to perform effectively on the job.

3. *Forbearance.* The manager of managers must also be willing to forego the luxury of blowing his or her top or berating assistants when things do go wrong. Delegation of authority requires that the manager of managers be discrete in criticism of subordinates who try to do things but fail in the process. Criticism of a subordinate will destroy morale and make people reluctant to shoulder responsibility. The manager of managers necessarily supervises people who may make mistakes because of the complexity of the decisions

that they are making. One can be assured that a subordinate *will* make some mistakes at some time or other, but the manager of managers who feels that he or she must make heads roll when things go wrong necessarily will be ineffectual.

4. *Self restraint.* Especially if he or she knows very much detail about the business, the executive must be able to exercise great powers of self restraint. Effective delegation at the management-of-managers level requires the manager to be content with exercising broad controls over results, to refrain from telling subordinates how to do a job or how to perform a specific task. It requires that the subordinate manager be given a degree of freedom and flexibility in deciding how a job will be done, when, and under what circumstances.

Policy-Making and Delegation by Managers of Managers

For the manager-of-managers to be effective as an executive, he or she must fulfill the following five requirements when delegating tasks:

1. *Policies must be stated clearly and explicitly.* Effective delegation at top levels of management requires that subordinates be able to operate within a framework of constraints. Of course any supervisor of supervisors will try to make decisions; however, these decisions must operate within the broad organizational constraints established by the manager of managers. For example, a supervisor of supervisors cannot schedule overtime if it is against corporate policy. Any manager of managers must clearly establish operating policies governing the situations which normally occur.

2. *Jobs must be defined.* All managers—direct supervisors, supervisors of supervisors, or managers of managers—deserve clear statement of the principal responsibilities for which they are to be held accountable. Once they know what their areas of operations are, by what they are constrained, and what is otherwise expected, then they can go ahead and try to accomplish these goals or objectives. Also, they can then be held accountable for performance on the job.

Unfortunately, many times people are not told exactly what they are to be held accountable for—and believe it or not, this also occurs at top echelons in organizations. The author is familiar with one manufacturing operation in which the vice president of manufacturing was unsure whether or not he had the authority to spend $200 for the repair of a machine which had broken down and which was critical to the ultimate performance of the job. Needless to say this vice president's morale was low, and work which should have been done was not accomplished because of his insecurity.

3. *Goals must be set.* Everyone likes to know how they're doing. This is especially true of people who get to be supervisors of supervisors or managers of managers in an organization. Practically everyone who rises to the higher positions in any organization will be motivated to achieve highly. Satisfaction of an achievement motive, by definition, requires knowing what (and when) one is achieving. That is, the individual must be aware of specific performance goals and objectives, what is considered good progress toward the accomplishment of those objectives, and what could be done to improve his or her performance. Any manager of managers knows that clear-cut definitions of performance goals and objectives are essential to success at the manager-of-managers level.

4. *Ideas must be communicated.* It is imperative that the central ideas underlying performance of the job be communicated to subordinates within the organization. Note that good delegators at the management-of-managers level do not tell their subordinates how to do things, but they do encourage both upward and downward communication between those subordinates and themselves (as well as laterally between people of the same level) in respect to ideas and activities which might be helpful in performing the jobs assigned.

5. *Controls for performance must be established.* The manager of managers must know what is being done, when it is being done, and whether or not what is being done is appropriate. Good delegation at the management-of-managers level thus requires that control points be established to ascertain whether or not satisfactory progress is being made toward the accomplishment of the objective. Good control is never easily attained, however, and doing so requires the establishment of certain guidelines such as the following:

- ☐ Clearly plan just what results are expected from delegating work to the subordinate.
- ☐ Plan regular inspection (or assessment of reports) of the action being taken by the subordinate to accomplish the delegated work.
- ☐ Be willing to take remedial or corrective action when necessary.
- ☐ Open channels of communication, both upward and downward, about any exceptional circumstances which may threaten completion of the delegated job.
- ☐ Develop a good recording or reporting procedure, designed to emphasize good *and* bad performance of the delegated work.
- ☐ Establish a definite schedule of times at which to review performance of the delegated work to determine whether it was done correctly, within established time constraints, and in accordance with organizational needs.

In any large organization, delegation at the top levels has requirements different from those of delegation at the lower levels. The reason for this is that the nature of the work being supervised by managers of managers is not the same as that of the work being supervised by direct supervisors or by supervisors of supervisors.

Remember that any manager's or supervisor's greatest obstacle to effective delegation lies in their not fully understanding what is expected of them at their organizational level when it comes to assigning work. While this chapter has devoted attention to that problem, it was designed to make the reader aware of the various problems that exist in different levels in the organization. Chapter 3 will also address the question of how one becomes more of a manager and less of a doer as he or she grows in the organization.

EXERCISES

1. Develop a detailed example of the changing patterns of delegation that any employee must go through in growing from a doer to a manager in your part of your organization. Be care-

ful to emphasize the time dimensions expected to be spent on "doing" versus "managing" functions. Also specify when you feel one becomes a supervisor of supervisors and a manager of managers.

2. Compare the steps that a manager of managers might take in making a delegation to the steps that a direct supervisor might take in making a job assignment!
3. Discuss the statement "It is more important that the direct supervisor have almost constant contact with his or her employees than it is for a manager of managers to have such constant contact."
4. When does delegation become abdication? Give an example. How might one check oneself as to whether he or she is abdicating?
5. Identify five indicators of effectively delegated work in your organization.
6. What would you consider to be the most essential function of a manager of managers in making effective delegations: (1) stating your policies, (2) defining jobs, (3) establishing goals, (4) communicating ideas, or (5) maintaining control over the work done? Why? Explain.

THE VITAL SHIFT FROM DOER TO DELEGATOR

As was pointed out in Chapter 2, successfully moving up through the managerial ranks in any organization creates special problems of delegation. Not only must the supervisor of supervisors and the manager of managers learn how to deal with subordinate managers who behave differently from the workers they have been supervising before, they must also make a basic change in their orientation toward giving work assignments.

This basic change is called "the vital shift" in management. Inability to make this vital shift severely limits both individual and organizational potential because failure to make the shift means that full utilization is not made of the human resources available in the organization. This chapter will devote its attention to the question of making the vital shift in management and the freeing of the manager's time so that he or she can do more important work, which is the ultimate goal of the delegation process.

WHAT IS MEANT BY "THE VITAL SHIFT"?

Managing managers and supervising supervisors is different from bossing workers or other nonmanagerial specialists. This is largely because the kind of individual who becomes a manager is entirely different—in personality and ambition levels—from the kind of individual who expects to be a rank and file employee throughout his or her working career.

Becoming a manager is no easy task, nor is it any kind of automatic condition which one necessarily grows into as one grows older. Whatever their educational, ethnic, or social background, people become managers primarily because they are ambitious. They want to get ahead, they have powerful drives for achievement and competition, and they need to excel. So they go into managerial jobs.

Except for those who have established their careers and are moving to new organizations, people are not usually hired directly into managerial jobs. Practically always they begin their employment at lower organizational levels, levels at which *functional* skills and abilities or specific *technical* talents are required. Thus individuals might be hired as engineers, accountants, machine operators, programmers, truck drivers, or what-have-you. Essentially they are hired because they are able to perform *mechanical tasks* which the employer is willing to pay to have done. They are expected to be highly competent at these tasks or to be able to learn. They are also expected to come to work, do their jobs well and in the prescribed fashion, take orders, and generally be "good" employees. Practically all the time they spend on the job they are doing something—driving a truck, programming computers, tending customers, and so on. Very little of their time, if any, is devoted to jobs which have to do with the management function. There is little or no responsibility for most rank-and-filers to plan their work (in a conceptual sense), get things organized, or check up on their progress. Of course, most employees will plan their work if the rudiments of planning are to be done, organize their tools and materials to (supposedly) best expedite the process, and monitor the operation of their machinery or equipment. However, these are not necessarily managerial functions. They do not involve other people.

Figure 3 illustrates graphically the relative amount of time spent by the typical rank-and-filer in the process of doing his or her job. It shows that by far the most time is spent doing technical work, with very little being spent on managerial or supervisory activities.* If individuals who are good employees also desire and intend to rise within the organization—becoming managers, shouldering more responsibilities, and making more money—they will invariably distinguish themselves. When that happens they may either ask or be asked to become supervisory personnel. Assuming that they are capable of shouldering managerial work responsibilities, they then become direct or line supervisors. In this capacity they begin to plan, schedule, coordinate, and control the activities of the people they are bossing. Now not only must they know what a good job is and how to do it, they must also be able to motivate the people who work for them to accomplish the job. Now, too, they must begin to assign work to various people on some kind of a basis that is acceptable to both the company and the employee.

---

* The ratios and quantities shown in all the figures in this chapter are purely arbitrary. They have been chosen simply to illustrate the point being discussed, and are not meant to be used as standards for any job.

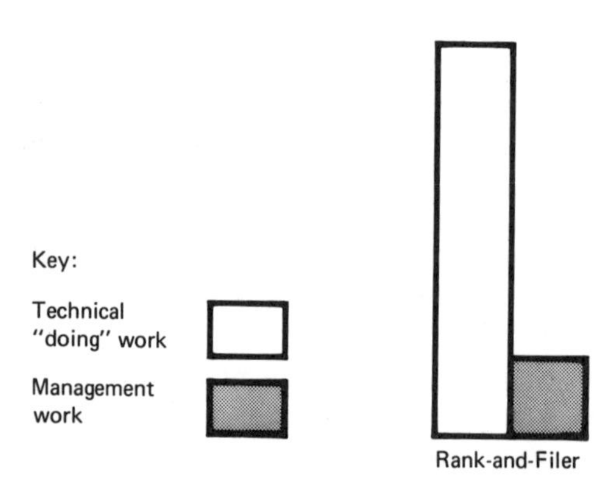

Figure 3

Handling managerial or supervisory responsibilities takes a great deal of time for the line supervisor. This is as it should be, because that is what he or she is being paid for—being a boss rather than a worker. When one shoulders these additional supervisory responsibilities, he or she should spend less time on the technical "doing" functions of the job. While the supervisor might well understand how to do the job he or she is supervising better than the subordinates who are doing it, the primary objective is to expedite that work; to ensure that the people who are supposed to do the work are actually doing it, that they have the requisite training skills and abilities to do it, and that the necessary supplies, materials, and machinery are available to them. This means that the amount of time which the supervisor should spend on the "doing" dimensions of the job should decrease and the amount of time spent on supervisory activities should increase. Figure 4 demonstrates the nature of this shift in emphasis.

As direct supervisors, individuals must begin to demonstrate their capabilities at organizing and planning and at pushing jobs through to completion. If they are successful at this, they will often be given yet greater responsibilities in the organization. Good managerial talent is always hard to find, and top-level management is always looking for people who can demonstrate competency at managerial skills.

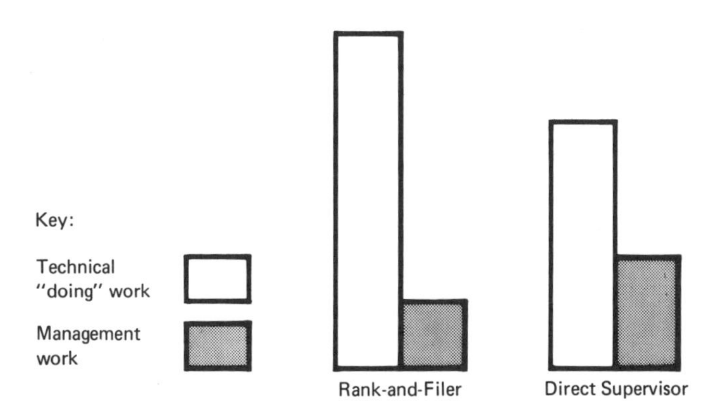

Figure 4

When an individual is promoted to the supervisor-of-supervisors capacity, additional managerial talents—as developed in Chapter 2—must be learned and applied. The supervisor of supervisors becomes a problem-solver and true coordinator of work activities. It is within his or her realm of responsibility to plan, coordinate, and control the activities of functional departments or other basic work units. In this capacity the supervisor of supervisors necessarily must become a true manager. In the words of Lawrence A. Appley of the American Management Association: "The job of the manager is to get results through people." Supervisors of supervisors definitely have this responsibility. They must get the work done and they must do so by getting others to do it. Not only must they get others to do the work, they must go through an intermediate level of supervision—the subordinate direct supervisor.

The supervisor of supervisors must have the talent of true coordinate skill. He or she must be able to see the big picture, must understand that at any given point certain things can go wrong, that problems will always be arising at various times within the organization. The supervisor of supervisors needs to devote more time to planning and scheduling, to coordinating and controlling people's activities, and less time to the "doing" aspects of the job. Figure 5 shows that relationship.

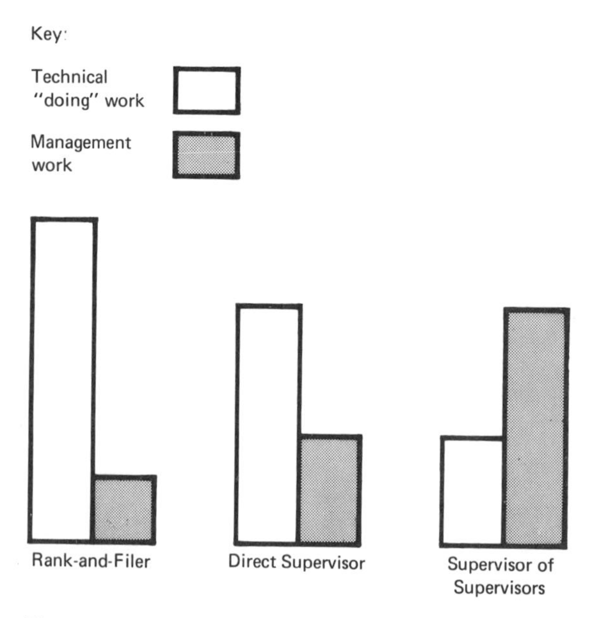

Figure 5

When one becomes a manager of managers the shift of emphasis on one's activities becomes more pronounced; there is still more time spent on managing functions and less on technical, "doing" functions. Indeed, when one becomes a manager of managers, one might really not "do" anything—at least nothing in respect to a functional, mechanistic task. The job of a top executive, or of those in the higher echelons of the organization, is almost totally to *manage*. In essence, their job is to know what needs to be done, not how to do it; they need to know the results desired and to be smart enough to hire people (as supervisors of supervisors) who know how the job is to be done. The supervisors of supervisors, in turn, must be smart enough to keep the direct supervisors going at expediting the job. And the direct supervisors, in turn, need to be smart enough to keep those responsible for doing the job, doing the job. Figure 6 shows this relative change of emphasis from mechanistic activities to managerial duties for the manager of managers.

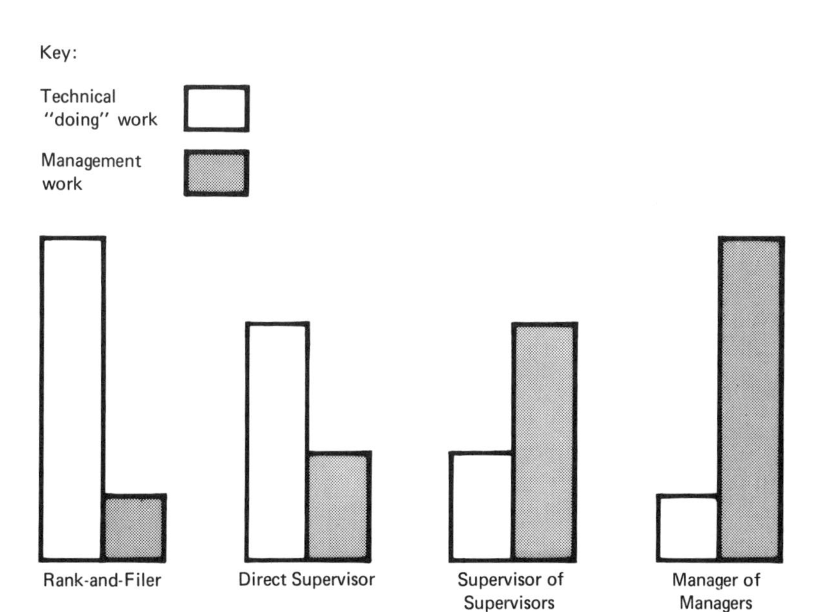

Figure 6

It should by now be clear that as one grows professionally as a manager he or she should spend less and less time on technical work and more and more time on managerial work. This shift in emphasis is referred to as the Vital Shift in Management—and it *must* be made if one is to grow professionally and develop his or her technical skills as a manager. Figure 7 demonstrate the nature of this shift in a rather dramatic form. Unfortunately, many managers fail to make this Vital Shift in Management—largely because they are poor delegators of work.

Most people find it difficult to see how their lack of skill at delegation limits their potential development as managers. They fail to understand that as one grows professionally one must spend more time managing and less time "doing," and that to spend more time managing means that the "doing" tasks must be farmed out to subordinates. As we stated earlier in this book, the objective of delegation is to free executive or managerial time. Let us consider a situation, though, that might make more clear-cut the importance

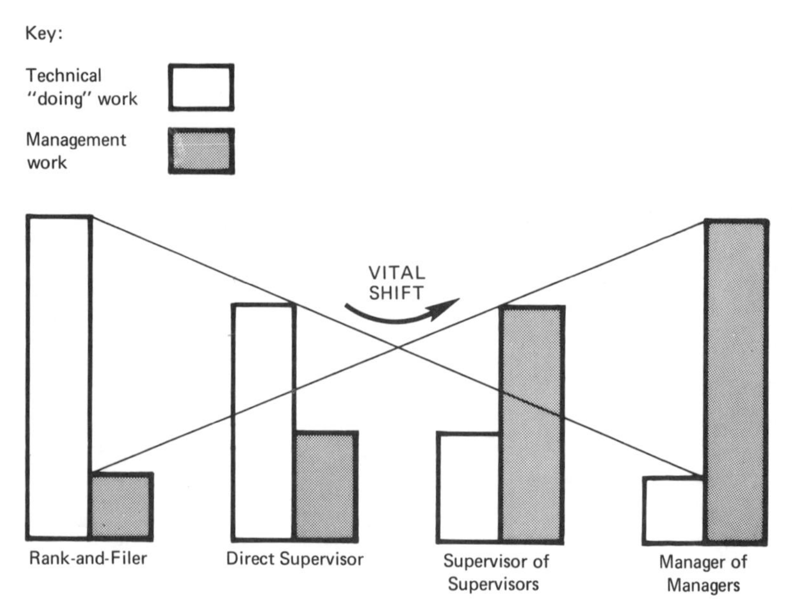

Figure 7

of this Vital Shift in Management and why, when failure occurs, the culprit is really inability to delegate upon the part of the manager.

THE DOER'S DILEMMA

Many people are hard working and ambitious. Hard working, ambitious people want to get ahead. Getting ahead, in the Western culture, practically always means rising to more responsible positions in an organization. A more responsible position in an organization necessarily means assuming supervisory or managerial roles. Therefore one can say that hard working, ambitious people want to become managers.

Traditionally our society has always rewarded hard work. The individual who is willing to devote long hours to training and skills-building is the one who ultimately gets the better job. The person who is willing to devote extra time and effort to performing the job is paid more. The individual who voluntarily shoulders responsibility is the one who gets "the nod" when plums are handed out by supervisors. Necessarily then, when a more responsible position becomes available, the best worker is picked to fill it.

Of course, promotion by this criteria alone could present problems, for while the best worker *may* be the best manager, he or she is *not necessarily* the best manager. A person could be tops in a "doing" job and just not have the knack for managing other people. Conversely, another person might be only moderately skillful at a "doing" job and still have superior talent and skill at managing people.

In any event, whoever is promoted to a supervisory position should be highly motivated and ambitious. Many times it is the supervisor's motivation and ambition that assure the successful completion of a job, but these qualities should not lead the supervisor into improper intervention. A hard-working, ambitious supervisor who sees his or her unit getting a little behind schedule may be likely to pitch in and help the workers produce, and while this is good for putting out fires and expediting matters, *it is not good management.* This is where people run into trouble with the Vital Shift in Management.

The supervisor's job is to manage and oversee the operations of his or her unit, and time spent in "doing" must be taken from the time which should have been spent managing. Faced with that problem, the hard-working supervisor may decide that the way around it is just to come in a little early in the morning and get things organized for the day. Or maybe stay a little late in the afternoon and get things set up for the next day. Or both. Now, that extra half hour at each end of the workday may not seem like much to the supervisor (who perhaps can rationalize that it helps him or her miss the peak traffic), but it means an extra five hours of work each week. Given a 40 hour work week, that's an increase in working time of 12½ percent. Unless the promotion included a pay raise of more than 12½ percent, the supervisor is now doing a more demanding and responsible job for an hourly pay no greater (and perhaps less) than he or she was getting as a rank-and-file worker. That's advancement?

Figure 8a shows the hypothetical technical-work/management-

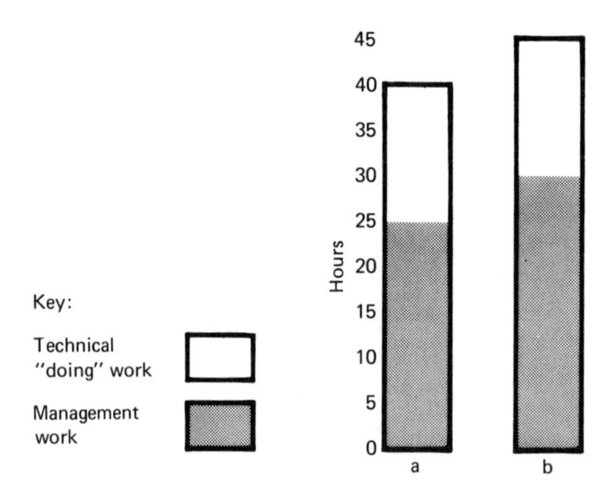

Figure 8

work ratio for a direct supervisor that was used in Figs. 4 through 7, but this time with the management work stacked on top of the technical work to represent a 40-hour week. Figure 8b shows what would happen in the case we've just been discussing; the supervisor has relinquished less of the technical work than he or she should but still has the same amount of management work to do. The only way to do it is to work more hours.

Suppose now that this same direct supervisor becomes a supervisor of supervisors and retains the habit of getting involved in extra technical work—perhaps not as much as before, but still too much. The proper (hypothetical) management-work/technical-work ratio used in earlier figures is shown in Fig. 9a. But our new supervisor has already been putting in an extra five hours a week and has a work week as seen in Fig. 9b. Now if our supervisor's responsibilities for managerial work grow still more, and if nothing is done about the amount of time spent on technical work, then this particular person is likely to see only one answer: work *even more hours* (Fig. 9c). When a crisis comes along, as they are bound to do now and then, he or she will work yet more hours. The pattern is thus established, and the time may very well come when

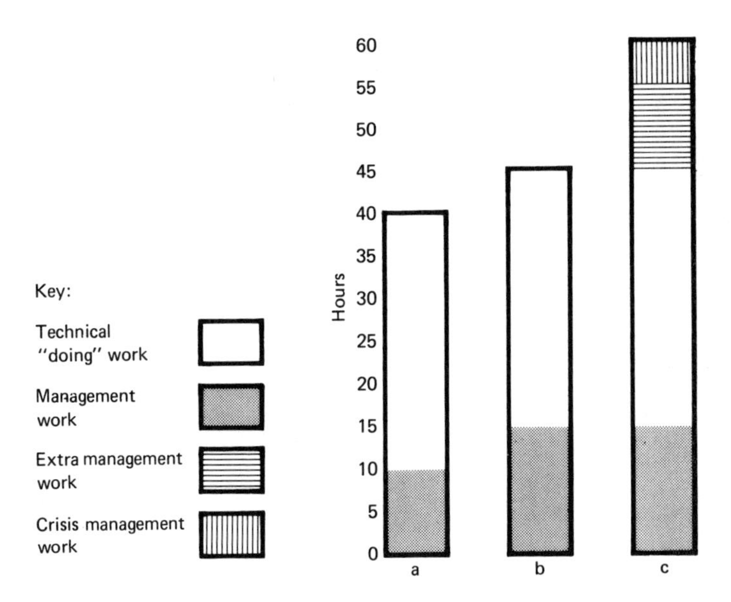

Figure 9

this administrator will find that 60, 70, or 80 hours a week are just not enough for the job.

Needless to say, at some point the supervisor of supervisors will reach the limit of the time that he or she can devote to the job without seriously affecting his or her life in other ways. Oftentimes the first tipoff comes when the supervisor, driving home late in the evening, wonders, "Where did all the time go?" Or it may come from the supervisor's spouse, with the earth-shattering statement, "You think more of that crummy job than you do of your family." Yet other times it is brought forcefully home by the manager of managers who almost literally stuns the supervisor of supervisors with, "You work damned hard around here, Charlie, but you're just not effective. Mary's getting the promotion instead of you because she seems to have things organized better."

It is very frustrating and depressing for a person to realize that the very thing he or she thought would bring success and advancement—the willingness to work hard and spend long hours at the job—has smashed those hopes. Yet it is not the *willingness to work hard* that blocks this person's ambitions, but the failure to recognize the fact that *when* one becomes a supervisor or manager, his or her prime responsibility is to *perform the necessary supervisory and managerial functions, not the technical, "doing" functions.* The latter must be delegated to the subordinates who are hired to do them. Thus the reader should understand that the very thing that may cause his or her success as a supervisor may also block that success. Always remember that managers manage, and doers do.

SAVING TIME—THE DELEGATOR'S REWARD

There are many reasons why managers fail to free up the time they could or should in their organization, but usually it is because they spend more time on "doing" functions than on managing functions. Of course it is hard to understand what one must or must not do at any given level in an organization. (We assume that it is only at the top levels of management that managers of managers perform practically no "doing" functions.) Direct supervisors and supervisors of supervisors are in the awkward stage of being "neither fish nor fowl"; they are expected to perform some "doing" functions. But which ones? A thorough study of things that managers do and don't do indicates that a good way to answer this question is to ask oneself, "Must I do this or could someone else do the job *sufficiently* well?" If the answer is, "Someone else could do the job *sufficiently* well," then somebody else *should* do it, not the supervisor or manager.

Rules for Good Time Utilization

A study conducted by High Yield Management, Inc., on how effective executives manage their time and delegate their work, developed a list of several rules and procedures commonly used by various managers, whether direct supervisors, supervisors of supervisors, or managers of managers. For the remainder of this chapter we will discuss these common approaches to the efficient utilization of time and how students of the art and skill of effective delegation can enhance their talents at being better managers, irrespective of their levels in their organizations.

Log Your Day One of the first things effective managers do, particularly when they feel that there isn't enough time in the day to devote to the things they must do in their managerial capacity, is to make a log of how they spend the major portions of their working day. Studies have proven over the years that the most common things that erode managerial and supervisory time include telephone calls, meetings, and uninvited and/or unnecessary visits by subordinates.

Many managers have found that by recording or logging how they spend the major portions of their working day they can control unnecessary drains on their time. Logging also lets them evaluate each activity on which they've spent significant amounts of time and determine which should be farmed out to someone else.

Schedule the Least Interesting Tasks when Your Energy is at its Peak Effective delegators of work tend to schedule their least interesting tasks when their energy is at its peak. People who put off unpleasant or unenjoyable jobs until their enthusiasm and energy are low find those jobs less pleasant than they need to be—and may even postpone them. But the things that are the most interesting to them, the most exciting and the most fun, they can do even when they *don't* feel much like working. So by scheduling their *least* interesting tasks when they feel *most* like working—whatever time of day that may be—they get a great deal more done.

This scheduling arrangement also causes them to assess whether or not they are doing things that should be delegated to someone else.

Avoid the Rolls-Royce Syndrome People oftentimes want to do or have the best. It must be recognized, however, that sometimes *the best is far better than is required.* It might be argued that the Rolls Royce is the finest quality auto in the world, but most people can fulfill their basic purpose in owning a car with something less expensive. The same principle applies in business and industry—

the best is often far better (and more expensive) than is needed for the purpose.

Keeping the Rolls Royce syndrome in mind, most good managers do not spend their time on things that someone else can do *sufficiently* well. Even if they can do a job better, there is no reason why they should spend any time on it unless the very best job is required.

Assign More Work than is Possible Effective managers of time and delegators of work purposely assign more work to their subordinates than the subordinates can accomplish. This way the subordinates are fully occupied and the manager does not have to break into his or her schedule so often to assign more work.

In assigning more work than they think is possible, managers essentially are acknowledging the validity of the old saying, "If you want something done, give it to a busy person to do." Though this may not sound logical, it seems that people who have the most to do also tend to get more done than those who have less to do.

Attack Long-Range Projects First Effective delegators of work attack long-range projects before short-time activities, getting their subordinates and employees started on the jobs that are expected to take longer to accomplish. This approach is based on the Zeigarnik effect, named for psychologist B. Zeigarnik, whose experiments on the influence of finished and unfinished tasks on individual behavior showed that most people have a built-in drive to complete or finish projects. Zeigarnik learned that unstarted work is not much of a motivator, but that unfinished work is a tremendous motivator. Thus when a manager tries to get his or her people started on long-range projects, he or she does so in an effort to "get the ball rolling," being confident that *once people get started* on a project, they have a tremendous and overwhelming drive to finish those projects.

Designate a Specific Time to Respond to Phone Calls and Read Mail Good managers realize that, on occasion, they must respond to telephone calls and read their correspondence. However, ineffective utilizers of time tend to respond to phone calls immediately and read mail as soon as it comes across their desk.

It is surprising how seldom it is urgent that one respond to any telephone calls other than those from superiors—and even then one sometimes wonders. One study found that better than 25% of the time spent on the telephone was in *waiting;* another study found that 44% of the telephone messages left in the organization studied would have turned out to be *of no consequence* if they had been left unheeded by their recipients.

In the same vein, the individual who feels compelled to read his or her mail as soon as it comes across the desk is probably an ineffective user of time and a poor delegator of work. Obviously direct supervisors seldom have anyone to sort their mail for them. However, once one does have a secretary it becomes a matter of course that the secretary should sort the mail, deciding just what things need to be brought to the attention of the boss and what things do not.

Avoid Emotional Attachment to that which is Irrelevant It is extremely common for poor delegators of work and people who are slovenly managers of their own time to get emotionally attached to the irrelevant. That is, they allow themselves to get bogged down in minute details and/or material not directly associated with getting the job done. The effects can be serious. As management expert George S. Odiorne has said, "Emotional attachment to the irrelevant will cripple an otherwise effective executive." The manager who can say, with David Farragut, "Damn the torpedoes. Full speed ahead!" will accomplish a lot more than the individual who complains, "My unit can't send that correspondence out because the postage machine is broken."

Arrange Task Priorities on the Importance of Task Goals Good delegators not only assign work to their subordinates, they also establish priorities for accomplishment, predicated on the importance of those task goals to the achievement of the unit. Studies have shown that poor delegators of work have a great deal of trouble assigning priorities to tasks because many times they don't know what is most important. Obviously, determining what is important and what is unimportant is a function of planning and control—a management function rather than a "doing" function.

Have Subordinates Respond to Messages and Telephone Calls, Draft Letters, etc. Effective delegators of work will, whenever possible, have subordinates attend to their correspondence and communications with others, both within and outside the organization. Many will carry this to the extreme by simply not responding to certain letters or by writing a reply on the original letter itself and making a copy of the result to return to the original sender.

Always Dispatch Paper that is Touched People who are extremely proficient in managing their time and delegating their work tend to feel that there are just three kinds of paper in their organization: (1) that which is simply for information and which can be discarded after it's read; (2) that which requires a completed response, such as making a telephone call, dictating a memo, etc.; and (3) that which may or may not require a response now, but in either case will require one at a later date. This kind usually ends up in the "pending" file for future attention. A good manager will act upon such paper so as to cause someone else to bring it to his or her attention *again* when the time is appropriate.

Schedule Meetings at the End of the Morning or Afternoon The conduct and control of meetings is extremely important to the effective management of time and delegation of work. Meetings can be a major cause of wasted time. Several ground rules have been developed over the years by people who know how to use meetings effectively. They include the following:

1. *Always use an agenda.* Good managers always make up an agenda for what is to be discussed at the meeting and never depart from it except for issues of the utmost importance.

2. *Set time limits for talking.* Many good managers will prescribe a specific time limit for discussion in an effort to preclude people from politicking. When President Gerald Ford appeared before the House Committee concerning itself with the Watergate investigation, each member of congress questioning him was limited to five minutes of inquiry not only to conserve the executives' time, but also in a not-completely-successful attempt to cut down on irrelevant discussion and politicking.

3. *Conduct meetings standing up.* Many managers who are

plagued with subordinates who get emotionally attached to the irrelevant, or otherwise don't know how to appropriately deport themselves in a meeting, have found that meetings usually are briefer and people tend to pay more attention if the meetings are conducted with everyone standing. People standing are less comfortable than when sitting, and so are more inclined to get to the point and get matters over with.

4. *Schedule meetings at the end of the morning or afternoon.* Studies show that meetings will end at noon or five o'clock *irrespective of when they start.* Good managers find that when a meeting is scheduled close to the end of the morning, afternoon, or work shift, people pay more attention and get to the subject quicker and easier than if the meeting were scheduled in the middle of the day, with ample time.

5. *Take chairs out of your office.* Many managers are plagued with people coming into their office (singly or in groups) and wasting time. The simplest solution is for the manager to remove from the office all chairs other than his or her own. As mentioned in item 3 above, people make their point sooner and more briefly when they must do so on their feet.

Use a Tickler File to Assure that Delegated Jobs are Done Most good managers establish a tickler file in which they jot down due dates, review dates, times to check on various projects which have been assigned to their subordinates, and so on. Usually they do this by noting the information on a calendar or memo pad so that *at an appropriate time in the future*—the right day or right week—they are reminded of it.

Review Budgets and Reports; Don't Make Them Good delegators of work avoid making up reports. They realize that their subordinates are the ones who are actually involved in doing the job and are the logical ones to report on what is happening or otherwise make up operating budgets. The effective executive will then synthesize portions of these budgets and reports as necessary for his or her own purposes.

Make Your Secretary or "Assistant to" a True Executive Assistant In recent years, many a company has set up a junior board of directors to act on decisions which the real board of directors is acting upon, the idea being that the junior board can compare its decisions with those made by the real board. In the same way, good developers of people often have their subordinates work on the same problems they are working on. This has the double purpose of training the subordinate to handle (and understand) management problems and developing the manager's confidence in the subordinate's ability. And it makes possible (from the viewpoint of both parties) the assignment of more complex tasks to the subordinate.

Never Touch a File Cabinet or any Other Tools An iron rule of many supervisors of supervisors and managers of managers is to never touch a file cabinet—or any other kind of "doers" tools. This maxim cannot be followed to the letter by direct supervisors because oftentimes they may have to maintain their own files. But they may not need to help out with tools. Once one has grown to the position of manager, he or she should never get involved in jobs requiring only "doing" skills.

Recognize that Training is the Best Investment in Terms of Human Resource Management Effective delegators of work realize that the only real limit on the work they can delegate to a subordinate is the type and amount of training that subordinate has had. Thus they spend a great deal of time and effort in preparing their subordinates to handle the assignments they are going to get.

Develop Controls One of the reasons many people fail at delegating work is that they are afraid that if they leave the job to someone else it might be done poorly or not be done at all. Yet good delegators of work are perfectly willing to assign to others work which might be vital to the delegator's very health and safety. For example, in the military, paratroopers do not usually pack their own parachutes; that work is assigned (delegated) to parachute riggers. Many people find this practice incomprehensible because of the criticality of correctness in the packing process. Yet parachute riggers do exist because adequate controls give them the incentive to do the job—and do it even better than would the individual who is going to actually make the jump.

Avoid Feelings of Guilt if You're not Busy As we will discuss later in this book, some managers fail at making work assignments because they feel guilty if they don't have anything to do. Consequently they try to retain work for themselves so they can be busy and convince themselves that they are efficacious and essential at work.

Don't Take on a Subordinate's Work Many managers fail to utilize their time effectively because they permit their subordinates to bring back to them work which was originally assigned to the subordinate. A job assigned to a subordinate should be done by the subordinate—who should be held accountable for it. More will be said about this later in the book. Suffice it here to say if the subordinate is permitted to bring questions and problems back to the superior and, *because of this,* the superior makes decisions for the subordinate, then the subordinate has effectively *delegated work back to his or her boss.*

Avoid Unnecessary Personal Inspections Many supervisors find that they must inspect what is going on. Inspection is, after all, a form of control. Homever, many people overcontrol, making repeated inspections which unnecessarily waste their time. Good managers avoid unnecessary inspections.

Don't Ask for Trouble Managers who ask subordinates what they can do to help them get their jobs done are too often told, in detail. Effective managers of time rely on the "exceptions" principle. That is, instead of trying to get their subordinates to tell them when things are going wrong (perhaps even when they aren't), they wait until the "exceptional" or "out-of-control" circumstances are brought to their attention by their subordinates.

The preceding checklist of ideas should help the effective manager in trying to utilize his or her time. Following the checklist will not necessarily make one a good delegator or assure all kinds of free time to devote to other management functions, but a basic application of the ideas behind those points can take one a long way toward being a more effective manager of time.

EXERCISES

1. What is meant by the "Doers Dilemma?" Is it a common problem in your organization? What are some examples of where it has existed for you in your career? How did you solve the dilemma? Were you right?
2. Do people that you work with or for commonly come in early or stay late? If so, why? Is this healthy for your organization? Why or why not?
3. What major problem is likely to be created by a direct supervisor who falls into the work habit of coming in early and/or staying late? Who is it most likely to hurt in the long run? Why? Can you think of any examples?
4. How can making a daily log of your work activities improve your delegation skills? Make a daily log for two weeks and then check your answer.
5. What is the Rolls-Royce syndrome? What job have you held that most often caused you to be victimized by the Rolls-Royce syndrome? How did you break out of it, or did you?
6. Keep a record of all the telephone messages you receive and analyze them to find how many were important and how many were wastes of time. What can you do about the time wasters?
7. From a mechanical sense, outline what it takes to have a good, effective meeting in respect to time, physical setting, conduct of the meeting, location, etc. Discuss your ideas in your next staff meeting. After the meeting, and with the help of your key subordinate, analyze how you handled the meeting. Well? Poorly? Both?

DELEGATION AT THE DIRECT-SUPERVISION LEVEL

As we have stated, the job of the direct supervisor is to get functional results from people. This requires the assertion of certain basic principles of management: The supervisor must: (1) make effective work assignments—clearly, concisely, and realistically, (2) obtain commitment from the subordinate to accomplish the established performance goals, and (3) follow up on the performance of the assignment.

MAKING EFFECTIVE WORK ASSIGNMENTS

For a work assignment to be effective, the superior and the subordinate must identify the subordinate's areas of authority and responsibility, establish standards of performance, determine priorities, and allow for a means of measurement.

Authority and responsibility. Certainly no one can perform a task effectively without knowing his or her areas of authority and responsibility—the matters he or she has control over and is accountable for. This requires that he or she understand clearly the objectives of the assignment and how they may be accomplished. (Depending on a number of factors, the "how" may sometimes be better determined by the subordinate than by the supervisor.)

The two basic means of communicating information in this and other work situations are by dialogue and by memo. Dialogue has the advantage of being immediate; both the giving of information and the receiving of feedback occur right *now,* with no delays. The supervisor can tell the subordinate whatever is necessary and, by questions, determine whether he or she was understood. The subordinate can also ask questions, acquire information, and make his or her own suggestions—all with a minimum of delay and confusion.

Memos can be cold, and they can even have a counterproductive effect if they are just dumped on the subordinate. This needn't be the case, though; they don't need to be stiffly formal and they should not be sent except when they will be useful. In essence, memos confirm in writing the things the supervisor and the subordinate have previously discussed, communicate new information or questions that do not require a right-this-minute response, and provide a handy way for one party to jog the memory of another person without bothering him or her.

Standards of performance. The supervisor must define very clearly to the subordinate just what standards of performance are to be observed for the job being assigned. It should be established just what is acceptable in matters of quality, quantity, and time scheduling. This applies to maximum criteria as well as minimum. As mentioned in an earlier chapter, performance beyond maximum requirements is uneconomical and unnecessary; not everybody *needs* to drive a Rolls Royce, however much they might want to.

Priorities. It may seem that one can set priorities for an assignment just by saying, "Do first things first," and it is true that this is often sufficient. Unfortunately, however, the first things are not always obvious—and the statement itself is not always valid. In some complex assignments the part or step that must be completed first may be very obscure (also, what may be clear to one subordinate may not be clear to another). Other assignments may require the completion of several parts or steps separately before progress can be made, in which case priorities may depend simply on what resources are most readily available. And in yet other assignments, important requirements outside the department could determine which part or step is completed first.

Measurements. Both performance standards and priorities should be established in such a way that they can be measured as the job progresses. The means of measurement may be mechanical, chemical, electronic, statistical, or what-have-you, but when considering standards and priorities the supervisor should keep asking himself or herself, "How can I measure the quality or progress of this step?"

OBTAINING COMMITMENT

If the goals or objectives of an assignment are to be achieved, the subordinate performing the assignment must be committed to them. The supervisor can help obtain that commitment in several ways. He or she can: be businesslike, focus attention on the expected results, be an active listener, solicit the subordinate's advice, and offer supervisory assistance. We will consider each of these suggestions in a little more detail.

Be businesslike. The subordinate will appreciate knowing that the supervisor considers the assignment important enough to discuss it thoroughly, including all the implications of what the supervisor is asking the subordinate to do. The supervisor should not, however, become involved in argument over methods or techniques. Good delegation of authority requires that the subordinate be given some freedom in determining how the job is to be done—within the limitations of quality control, customer requirements, etc.

Focus attention on expected results. As established earlier, the subordinate should be thoroughly briefed on what is expected of him or her in the performance of an assignment, as well as when and how it is expected. But the supervisor should not forget that it is a person who will be doing the job, not a machine, and that person has certain interests, likes and dislikes, strengths and weaknesses. The supervisor should try to help commit those interests, likes, and strengths toward the assignment.

Be an active listener. The subordinate should have the opportunity to express his or her fears or concerns and raise questions on points about which he or she is uncertain. The supervisor should be interested in such matters and let the subordinate see that interest. In dealing with the questions raised by the subordinate, the supervisor should clearly explain what performance is expected of the subordinate, how it will be measured, and what problems might be anticipated.

Solicit the subordinate's advice. In making an assignment, it's a good idea for the supervisor to solicit advice from the subordinate about what might be done, how it might be done, what obstacles might be expected, and what might make it easier for the subordinate to accomplish the objective. There are at least three good reasons for doing this: it will expedite achievement of the goal; it will improve the working relationship between the supervisor and the subordinate; and as often as not the supervisor will learn something from it.

Offer supervisory assistance. Unless the supervisor is what is known as a "working supervisor," he or she does not offer to help with the "doing" part of the assignment; to do so would cancel the purpose in assigning the job to the subordinate. But the supervisor should offer whatever help the supervisory position can provide in the form of authority, information, etc. This is not only good for the subordinate's morale, in showing that he or she has the supervisor's backing, but it also expedites the completion of the job.

FOLLOWING UP ON THE ASSIGNMENT

As pointed out in earlier chapters, it is essential that the direct supervisor follow up on work assignments to ascertain how they are being accomplished. In this case, good follow-up requires that the supervisor apply the following basic procedures as they become appropriate.

Discuss the subordinate's job performance with him or her. It is important for the direct supervisor to discuss with the subordinate his or her impression of how well or poorly the subordinate is doing on the assignment. The supervisor should be honest and open with these assessments, citing examples of what constitutes good or bad performance, but should *not* be harsh or destructive. Tactfulness is essential in criticism. It is a good idea to hold these discussions at the subordinate's place of work, for he or she is likely to feel most comfortable there.

Don't get personal. The supervisor should *never* attack the subordinate's personality, character, or attitudes. It is the subordinate's job performance that is being examined, and the supervisor should stick to the subject. Also, the time is the present, and the supervisor should not dwell on any problems that may have occurred with the subordinate in the past.

Assess performance by established standards. We have mentioned that performance standards for a job should be established when the job is assigned. It is important that the supervisor stick to these standards in assessing the subordinate's performance. The subordinate is not in competition with other employees, and his or her performance should not be pitted against theirs. Nor should it be compared with how the supervisor thinks he or she would have done the job.

Keep an open mind. When the subordinate has not performed the assignment to standard, the supervisor should determine whether there are mitigating circumstances that would justify the lapse. Sometimes conditions or requirements do change and prevent the subordinate from meeting the standards.

Be careful about giving advice. When the subordinate gets off the track, as will sometimes happen, and fails to perform the assignment as required, the supervisor should *not* just take over and tell the subordinate every move to make. That may get the job back on schedule, but it has three negative effects: (1) Essentially, it becomes the supervisor who is doing the job, rather than the subordinate to whom it was assigned. That's not good delegation. (2) It does not improve the subordinate's morale or self-confidence to see that the supervisor thinks him or her incapable of handling the assignment. That's not good personnel relations. (3) The subordinate will learn something by watching the supervisor straighten things out—but not nearly so much as if he or she had been guided and helped to work out the solution for himself or herself. And that's not good training.

Certainly the supervisor has the responsibility to keep the assignment moving on schedule, but it will be better for the subordinate, the department, and the company if he or she can do so by *guiding* the subordinate to the solution, rather than otherwise.

Face up to failures. There's many a successful person who can truthfully say, "I wouldn't be so successful now if I hadn't failed in the past—and learned from it." The good supervisor (at any level) will recognize failure, accept it, and learn from it. The solution may involve new training for the subordinate (or for the supervisor), it may mean some reorganization, or it may mean any of a number of other things. But it is a learning situation, and usually both the supervisor and the subordinate can profit from it.

Recognize progress. Certainly it is a good idea to make a favorable comment when a subordinate is performing above the standards set for an assignment. It is also sound to acknowledge when he or she is performing right at standard. When the job is on schedule, when the quantity and quality of work are what they should be, then progress is being made—and the subordinate will be glad to know that the supervisor recognizes that fact.

TAILORING SUPERVISORY STYLE TO THE NEEDS OF SUBORDINATES

Currently, personnel management is largely based on the Contingency Theory of leadership, which assumes that one's effectiveness at leadership depends on many things: whether the supervisor has authority to command the subordinate; whether the subordinate accepts or rejects that authority; and the circumstance in which the supervisor and the subordinate find themselves.

This was not always so. In the 1930's and 1940's the Human Relations Movement taught that the supervisor should be deeply concerned about whether his or her subordinates were happy, had interesting work, and approved of their working conditions. While these are still valid interests of management, it eventually became clear that they were not the whole answer; happy employees, for example, do not automatically become optimum producers—some prefer just to be happy.

In the 1950's and 1960's the Revisionist Theory of Management came to the fore. McGregor's theory Y became popular, claiming that the supervisor should feel that all employees would demonstrate drive, initiative, and creativity toward organizational goals under the right circumstances. The real problem for the supervisor, argued theory Y, was to define clearly to the subordinate what was necessary to maximize performance—and to obtain commitment to that performance from the subordinate. It has been demonstrated that while explaining goals does improve performance, it does not necessarily guarantee commitment. Some employees might have other objectives in mind, and some of those who were committed to the stated goals might be blocked from them by physical constraints such as lack of time, funds, materials, and so forth.

The 1970's saw the development of the Contingency Theory, already mentioned, and it is very likely that this theory will remain popular with those who understand the problems of direct line supervision. It is probable, therefore, that direct supervisors of the next several years will need to modify their supervisory style to meet the needs of their subordinates. The remainder of this chapter will discuss some of the problems of this approach, considering such things as: different degrees of supervisory authority; how management by exception is a basic principle that facilitates effective delegation; how the supervisor can correct the performance of subordinates without demoralizing them; and how the supervisor can live with subordinates' differences of opinion about how jobs should be done.

Degrees of Supervisory Authority

Supervisory authority may vary between companies or between departments in the same company. These variations in authority can (though they may not) affect the attitude of subordinates toward their supervisors. To illustrate the point, consider a military organization on the one hand and a volunteer social-service organization on the other. Subordinates in the former are likely to take orders from their superior with a minimum of hesitation or discussion; subordinates in the latter may actually be able to dictate the job conditions to their supervisor. Of course, this example uses extremes, but we will now discuss degrees of authority in the more commonplace situation of the civilian working for a living.

The Supervisor has Little or no Power In some work situations subordinates feel that their boss has little or no power in the organization. When this is the case, subordinates often feel that they have more power than the direct supervisor. Characteristically, they then resent being given orders and often rebel (usually successfully). This is likely to be chronic in a volunteer or loosely organized job situation. It becomes acute when subordinates know they can not easily be replaced because of their job skills or because there are no available replacements in the work force. In these circumstances the subordinates almost always choose their own goals and the methods of achieving them. Oftentimes their attitude is one of out-and-out resistance to and categorical rejection of work assignments given to them by their boss.

Coping with indifference. In the situation just described, the supervisor must demonstrate talent as a *laissez faire* supervisor; he or she must not be in any way dictatorial or autocratic. Prudent bosses may try to sell ideas, at best. More commonly, they will look toward the subordinate for suggestions as to what it is that the subordinate expects to do. This is not abdicating supervisory responsibilities; rather, it gives the supervisor the chance to use moral suasion, relying on the fact that most people will try to do a reasonably good job *if they want to.* In this situation, subordinates often respond well to frank, open discussion of why they want (or do not want) to do something.

While genuine contempt for the boss's power is commonly seen where volunteer subordinates are concerned, it is not so common when the subordinates are actually being paid and working for a living. Practically always the supervisor has the ultimate option of seeking the discharge of a subordinate who is totally disrespectful of organizational needs. Therefore, genuine laissez faire supervisory styles are very seldom needed.

The Supervisor has Moderate Power In the more common power situation subordinates usually perceive their bosses as having some degree of power, power which is backed up by the ultimate possibility of their discharge for failure to comply with the boss's wishes. However, as discussed earlier in this book, oftentimes a leader has only that power bestowed by his or her subordinates.

In this more common situation it is usually true that subordinates do expect—and appreciate—having some control over the methods they will be using in doing the work assigned to them. They simply want to have some control over their work—the methods, sequences, techniques, etc. It makes the job more personal and more satisfying. In these work situations subordinates show a strong "middle-class" set of values. Invariably they like the system in which they are operating, but they are not especially keen on having someone pull rank or exert any strong authority over them. Employees in this circumstance will practically always show a tremendous desire to have a say in what they are going to do. This is especially true when their skills are relatively scarce on the job market.

Bureaucratic, democratic, and participative methods of management. When the direct supervisor has some authority, but not a lot, he or she should adopt one of three behavior patterns: democratic, bureaucratic, or participative. The democratic style, of course, relies heavily on having subordinates offer their suggestions about what should or should not be done. Employees feel free to express their opinions, but they defer to the wishes of the majority.

In the bureaucratic situation, the leader usually lets the organization superimpose its constraints on what the individual must be required to do. In this case the supervisor is dealing with strength, but nevertheless is not insisting that the employee unthinkingly follow commands without any questions.

In the participative circumstance, employees are solicited for their opinions on what they should do, and how and under what circumstances they should do it. The leader tends to recognize that his or her power to tell people what to do is relatively limited. Consequently, he or she will use power with restraint, being more inclined to defer to the wishes of the group. The participative leader necessarily tries to get consensus among his or her subordinates on what they're going to do, how they're going to do it, and what the final outcome can be expected to be.

In the above situations, of course, the leader has some sanctions that can be applied if people fail to perform. However, the best way for the supervisor to obtain compliance with his or her wishes—and the least painful for all concerned—is to stay on top of his or her own job and be well supplied with knowledge and information of value to the subordinate.

The Supervisor is Perceived as Being Quite Strong Research by Dr. Charles Hughes of Texas Instruments has shown that some employees are virtually tribalistic in their attitudes and feelings toward "the boss" and what he or she can do. They believe the boss to be almighty in his or her power and authority—*even* *though this belief may be mistaken.* These people are essentially dependent on their leader and apparently have a tremendous psychological need to be told—or otherwise guided to do—what is expected of them. In their eyes a good leader is decisive, firm, and opinionated. About the only demands they make upon the leader is that he or she look out for their general welfare.

At one time or another almost everybody has experienced situations in which a leader was extremely power-oriented—and they often found that having a strong, autocratic leader was not all that bad. For example, if a multi-engine commercial aircraft should lose power in one engine, the pilot (leader) decides autocratically whether to continue to the planned destination, choose an auxiliary objective, or return to point of origin. Passengers will not be given the opportunity to assert any strong opinion on the matter, nor do they wish to do so. Practically always they are content to defer to the pilot's judgment, experience, and expertise. Now, while this example does not show a direct supervisor-to-subordinate kind of relationship, the point is clear that in some cases it is virtually imperative that someone take command and tell others what to do, how to do it, and where to do it. This need practically always arises in emergency situations. Many organizations experience similar crises in terms of getting jobs done, getting the work out, or otherwise conducting their duties.

Living with power. Any leader who is perceived to be in a very strong, powerful position will tend to be dictatorial or autocratic in his or her behavioral patterns. Practically always they find that such behavior is expected of them. If they fail the subordinates' need to be told, they will usually find that work is not done, or not done the way it should be.

Many leaders find it antithetical to their nature to be directive; they simply don't like telling other people what to do, no matter what. However, when a leader finds himself or herself in a position in which the subordinate expects to be told, then he or she had better assume an autocratic or dictatorial style. Making effective work assignments in these situations requires telling individuals what they are to do rather than guiding them into deciding it for themselves.

Assessing Management by Exceptions

Those leaders who find themselves in varying situations of power must recognize that managing by exception is probably the single most valuable managerial tool available to them. According to management expert Franklin G. Moore, the exception principle helps supervisors and executives to avoid being bothered with burdensome detail. What is meant by "the exception principle" is just this: The supervisor establishes rules for subordinates to follow in routine or repetitive situations; the subordinates come to the supervisor for guidance only when the circumstances are not covered by the rules.

Since many of the activities at the "doing" level are routine or repetitive, this procedure will save much of the boss's time—and it will help ensure that policies are carried out in a consistent fashion. In establishing specific rules governing the performance of regular, workaday, routine functions, the direct supervisor is necessarily defining the subordinate's decision-making jurisdiction—and giving him or her the license to make those decisions that fall within it. When things come up which do not fit the rules, these "exceptional" circumstances can (and should) be brought to the attention of the supervisor.

Note that when the supervisor resolves exceptional circumstances, he or she may well be defining *new* policies and operational rules within which the subordinate can function *in the future.* Thus the supervisor can delegate increasing decision-making capabilities and responsibilities to immediate subordinates. This, of course, means that the subordinate assumes more and more work responsibilities, thereby freeing the supervisor's time for the more important management functions for which he or she is responsible.

What to do when Mistakes Occur

Almost without fail, when a supervisor gives a subordinate a job assignment, mistakes will occur. Somewhere along the line work doesn't get done or some other sort of problem develops. When these things happen it is a very common reaction for supervisors to want to "blow their stack" or otherwise raise hell with the employee involved. But it was pointed out earlier that an effective delegator of work must resist the temptation to lose his or her temper.

Another temptation that the supervisor must avoid is that of getting personally involved in correcting the error. Correcting the error itself is not a supervisory function; it is the responsibility of the subordinate to perform the task the way it should have been done in the first place. Correcting the *cause* of the error is not a supervisory function; it is the responsibility of that department which handles training and development. If training and development are not sufficient, it may be necessary to redefine performance expectations for the employee involved—and the possibility must be considered that he or she may simply not be working up to capacity.

In attempting to cope with mistakes and errors being committed at work, the direct supervisor should determine *why* the mistake occurred and *why* the employee was unable to dispatch his or her duties properly. Some of the more common reasons (though there are others) are as follows:

- ☐ Too much work was dumped on the person at one time.
- ☐ The individual was required to do too much, too fast.
- ☐ The individual did not fully understand what was required.
- ☐ Performance expectations were unrealistic.
- ☐ Contingencies were not provided for.
- ☐ Overall performance expected from the subordinate, and how various details of the job fit into these overall expectations, were not explained properly.
- ☐ Progress toward the accomplishment of objectives was not monitored.
- ☐ Unanticipated problems were not provided for.

If the supervisor accepts these items as fairly realistic indicators of why things were not done, or were done incorrectly, he or she should be in a position to tactfully discuss those inadequacies with the subordinate and inspire that person to remedial or corrective action. The supervisor who resorts to "scream and scare 'em" tactics at this stage will find that his or her subordinates will become uncooperative, demoralized, and oftentimes out-and-out resistant toward work responsibilities.

Living with Differences of Opinion

Inevitably, in making work assignments, there will be a difference of opinion between the supervisor and the subordinate about whether the latter can or even should do a particular job. While a worker's obstinancy or flat refusal to do a job will inevitably require being dealt with in a firm manner, it is important for the supervisor to recognize when there is a genuine difference of opinion. When the worker and the direct supervisor genuinely disagree, but just as genuinely want to resolve their differences of opinion, the best way to cope with the problem is by methods suggested by Drs. Alan C. Filley and Robert J. House. They are:

1. There must be little or no expression of personal, self-oriented needs by the individuals involved in the conflict.
2. The self-needs that *are* expressed by people involved in the conflict must be satisfied through the course of the discussion of what must be accomplished by the organization.
3. There must be a generally pleasant atmosphere and the participants must recognize the need for unified action.
4. The group's problem-solving activity must be not only understandable but also orderly and focused on only one issue at a time (assuming that more than one issue is at conflict).
5. The facts surrounding the problems and differences of opinion must be available and must be used in the problem resolution.
6. The boss, through tactful and careful probing, must help the subordinate or subordinates to analyze why they feel the way they do about the problem.
7. The direct supervisor and his subordinate or subordinates must feel personally friendly toward each other.*

---

* Filley, Alan C., and Robert J. House, *Managerial Process and Organization Behavior*, Glenview, Ill.: Scott, Foresman, 1969, p. 317.

Needless to say, it's difficult to meet all these conditions. It takes an extraordinarily tactful direct supervisor to even deliver his or her side of those requirements. In a situation in which many subordinates are contemptuous of their boss and view him or her as having little or no power (as discussed earlier), it is likely that the subordinates concerned will refuse to adopt the required attitude for effective resolution of conflict. When conflict cannot be resolved, it must be controlled by the supervisor. If the supervisor is in a position to behave autocratically, then the job will be relatively easy (although the results may not be desirable). Invariably, more effective supervisors prefer to adopt an "I win/you win" solution rather than rely on power to force an issue.

The more successful supervisors adopt an "I win/you win" attitude because they have found that if they adopt an "I win/you lose" attitude toward a subordinate, then the subordinate will, intuitively, adopt an "I win/you lose" attitude toward the supervisor. The subordinate takes the position that "You may win on the point of conflict because you are the boss, but you'll lose on something else because *I'll get you later.*" Necessarily, when both sides have an "I win/you lose" attitude, somebody *has* to lose. Unfortunately, when people find themselves in a position from which they have little or no hope of winning, they often adopt an "I lose/you lose" attitude—"I'm going to lose, but I'm going to make you lose too." When this happens, very little of a constructive nature is achieved; results are desultory at best. Therefore, when experienced supervisors encounter differences of opinion between themselves and their subordinates, they adopt the attitude, "How can we resolve this circumstance for the good of *all* involved, the organization, the subordinate, and the supervisor?"

EXERCISES

1. Tape-record a session in which you are actually making a real delegation or a job assignment to one of your subordinates. Critique your performance before your training group at a later time, along the following dimensions:

a) Did you define the general area of responsibility clearly? How might you have done better?

b) Did you establish priorities of work and how success was to be measured, as well as *when?* How might you have done better?

c) Did you really get commitment from your subordinate? What evidence do you have that you did (or didn't)?

d) What are your plans for follow-up? Write these plans down. Set a meeting time to review with your study group how the follow-up plans were implemented.

5

BARRIERS TO EFFECTIVE DELEGATION AT THE DIRECT SUPERVISION LEVEL

There are many reasons why line supervisors fail at effectively delegating or assigning work to their subordinates. One of the continuing themes of this book is that these reasons fall into two basic classifications: (1) the boss is inept at or incapable of making effective work assignments; (2) the subordinate to whom the work has been delegated or assigned somehow, in some way, manages to avoid doing it. This chapter will examine why direct supervisors are sometimes ineffective at making work assignments, and why, if they are effective, some subordinates do not perform the assignment as they should.

WHY SUPERVISORS FAIL TO DELEGATE

Some direct supervisors fail to delegate because they simply don't know how to issue orders to their subordinates or effectively communicate with them. It should be recognized, however, that most of the barriers to good delegation are psychological in nature; many of them resulting from the line supervisor's inability to cope with the problems he or she experiences in making the vital shift from a doer to supervisor and, ultimately, to manager. Let us examine some of the more common psychological reasons why line managers fail, or at least are often inept, at making effective work assignments.

"I Can Do It Better Myself"

This is one of the most common psychological reasons why direct supervisors sometimes fail to assign work to their subordinates. Sometimes the supervisor *can* do the job better, but more often he or she cannot. In fact, one study conducted by the author indicates that in about 80% of the cases in which supervisors say "I can do it better myself," they are mistaken. Of that 80%, *all* the subordinates can do the job as well as the supervisor, and several of them can do it better. This is true whether the assigned task involves handling hardware or abstractions or people; most of the time the subordinates can do the job as well as the supervisor.

But what if the supervisor *can* do the job better than the subordinate to whom it would be assigned? Well, it's the Rolls Royce syndrome all over again: If one person can do a job *as well as necessary*, it is just plain wasteful of time, money, energy, and material to have someone else do it *better than necessary*. Besides, the time the supervisor spends on a job that could be done by a subordinate, while it is productive, means that an equivalent amount of supervision or management time has been lost to the company.

Certainly it is easy for us all to be fooled into feeling that we could do the job better, and it's no shame to recognize that fact; personal pride misleads us, and of course it is always easier to see another person's shortcomings than to see our own. But most of the time any supervisor who knows his or her subordinates can make a work assignment with confidence that it will be done every bit as well as it should be.

Inability to Give Instructions

Of course a supervisor should cover every detail of a job with the subordinate to whom it is being assigned. But even then the supervisor could fail to make an effective job assignment because he or she may not: (1) be able to give orders effectively or (2) have a clear understanding of what he or she needs to have done.

Inability to give orders can result from several things. The supervisor may fear that the subordinate will: (a) think the supervisor lazy for not doing the work himself or herself; (b) think (and maybe show it) that the supervisor is trying to get out of doing a dirty job; or (c) reject the supervisor, openly or covertly. Or it may be that the supervisor has a handicap, such as a speech impediment or difficulty in writing or a serious lack of facility with words. Or he or she may be overaggressive in speech and manner, a quality that puts many people off.

The supervisor who feels that he or she is unable to give orders effectively must work on that handicap, must assess what the problems or difficulties are. One way to do this, of course, is to check oneself out with someone on the same or higher level in the organization. Defensiveness is a killer; openness and frankness go a long way toward enabling the supervisor to recognize what the problems are. And recognizing the problems is the most essential step to overcoming them.

The supervisor who doesn't know what he or she needs to have done cannot really assign work to a subordinate (unless he or she is willing to accept whatever the subordinate comes up with). The importance of precisely defining job performance expectations for the subordinate was discussed in some detail earlier, so we needn't go into that again at this time. But any supervisor who feels that people act as if they don't *understand* what he or she wants done should examine just how precisely and accurately he or she is defining performance expectations for the subordinates in terms of quantity, quality, and timeliness or scheduling.

Bias

Many supervisors, particularly those at the direct line level, oftentimes fail at delegating work and/or effectively utilizing the human resources available to them because of bias or bigotry. The person who is biased usually does not recognize the fact, and, indeed, commonly feels that his or her attitude is fully justified—even commendable. And we sometimes see or hear a deeply bigoted person arguing loudly—and with apparent sincerity—against bigotry. In situations of overt bias, the overtly biased individual, however, is often aware of the problem to some degree but simply may not be inclined to do anything about it.

The supervisor who is prejudiced against certain minority groups—blacks, chicanos, orientals, etc.—may very well know that he or she doesn't trust, appreciate, or understand the minority group member and therefore is reluctant to assign responsible work to him or her. In other cases the problem is more subtle and, for that reason, *probably more severe.* It might not be a question of reluctance to assign responsible work to the object of one's prejudice; rather it may be a malicious act in which the supervisor *does* assign work to that person—dirty work.

Forms of prejudice other than racial also exist. For example, women are a minority in the work force and for years have been discriminated against in job opportunities, responsibilities, and salaries. The women's liberation movement has made a concerted effort to get rid of these and other areas of discrimination in employment.

Unfortunately, a lot of people (women, as well as men) don't recognize that they are biased against the opposite sex. This author has many times heard men say that they are not really biased against women doing certain jobs. Yet many of those men look a little sheepish when they are asked, "How would you feel if you discovered, at an altitude of 25,000 feet, that the pilot of your airplane was a woman?" or "How did you feel when you found out the bellhop at your hotel was a woman?" or "How did you feel the first time you saw a woman driving a truck?"

And who among us does not show bias at some time or other? Which of us has not, on occasion, thought something like: "Fred's a good man because he grew up on a farm," or "Fred's kind of an odd ball because he grew up on a farm." And how many readers have *never* asked a job applicant such questions as: "Where did you grow up?" "Where did you go to school?" "What do you like in music, clothing, etc.?" These questions all show bias, and such attitudes often make supervisors reluctant to utilize effectively the human resources available to them—because they are biased *in favor* of people who, say, grew up in the same circumstances they did and against those who didn't. And all the time it really doesn't matter whether the subordinate is white, black, brown, yellow, red, or striped; is male, female, or physically one and emotionally the other; was born in this country or another; or was raised in the city, the country, or a tree. All that should matter to the supervisor is, "Will he (or she) do the job as it should be done?"

Poor Controls and Follow-Up

Any good supervisor will be reluctant to delegate work to a subordinate unless he or she can be sure that the job will be done right. And in order to be sure, the supervisor must have good control over the work and insist that subordinates follow certain minimum standard procedures. Though this may sound a bit difficult, it can be done even under widely varying conditions, as anyone can testify who has ever eaten at a place where food is prepared and sold commercially. All such places, from the lowliest quick-food outlet to the most luxurious dining salon, are subject to certain laws and regulations. True, some of these places, at all levels, meet established requirements better than others, but the system works well enough so that, with all the millions of meals and snacks served commercially in this country in a year's time, remarkably few people suffer ill effects from anything but overindulgence.

The supervisor may find that some controls and/or follow-up procedures already exist, and that, with a little imagination, he or she can think of enough others to ensure that the assigned job will be done as and when it should be. Or it may be that the supervisor will have to develop such a system from scratch. But whatever the situation, the supervisor who says, "I can't delegate work because I have no assurance that the job will be done correctly," is simply admitting incompetence as a delegator, or is so unimaginative that he or she will never be a truly effective supervisor.

Fear of Being Shown Up

This particular fear is especially acute in the minds of those who have come up through the ranks in an organization, particularly if they have been especially proud of their skill at their job. It's difficult enough for such people to see others take on the responsibility for jobs that were theirs to forego the pleasure of actually being involved. But it's more difficult for the new supervisor to recognize that the subordinate not only can probably do the job satisfactorily but, indeed, may actually do the job *better* than he or she did. The boss may then feel that his or her reputation is at stake and be very reluctant to let the subordinate do the job—even, sometimes, finding all sorts of excuses and reasons why the work cannot be assigned to the subordinate.

Any boss who is reluctant to delegate work to a subordinate through fear that the subordinate will outshine him or her not only does not demonstrate good managerial judgment, but also probably should not even consider being a boss for very long. Good bosses invariably delight in—at least capitalize on—subordinates who can outperform them. Many very successful managers have said that they did not possess the skills to build businesses or manage industries themselves, but were *smart enough* to harness the talents of those who *did* have such skills. Supervisors who are afraid of the subordinate who can outperform them necessarily will never grow to become supervisors of supervisors or managers of managers.

Uncertainty of Authority

Many supervisors fail to delegate work to subordinates because they are not sure that they have the authority to make such assignments. The first chapter of this book addressed the question of authority and the four forms of authority: position, competence, personality, and character. It was argued that people really *do* have the authority to do things that they want to do unless it is *specifically* withheld from them. A supervisor may not be authorized to cash a check or carry the keys to the building, but aside from such mechanistic matters, should certainly have the authority required to do the job with which he or she has been charged.

Supervisors who argue that they do not assign certain jobs to certain individuals because they're not authorized to do so should have very clear evidence to back up that claim. Otherwise they are simply playing ostrich to their responsibilities as direct line supervisors.

The Guilt Drive

Some line supervisors don't want to (or can't) delegate work to subordinates because they will feel guilty about not having anything to do themselves. This particular psychological hang-up is not common among supervisors, but where found, it is often chronic.

The problem with the guilt drive is that it causes some people to have the overwhelming urge to always be busy. They have learned, as children, that "Satan finds mischief for idle hands," "An idle mind is the devil's workshop," and other such bits of folk wisdom. It should be obvious that this particular psychological block to effective delegation is simply a misinterpretation of what the word "work" means. To a construction worker it means hard physical labor; to a theoretical mathematician it means intense mental concentration—and the one may be as tiring as the other. To the supervisor's subordinate, "work" means what we have called a "doing" activity; to the supervisor it *should* mean managing other people and resources—each of them has a separate course to follow to get a given job done *most effectively*.

The supervisor who is afraid that his or her boss might catch him or her with "nothing" to do is feeling guilty, and will "do" things just to be busy. This is not desirable, since at the very least it takes time from managing. But would many of us want to have our boss catch us doing nothing? Probably not. So most of us feel we must keep busy. Putting the question to ourselves like that it becomes obvious that we all suffer a little bit from the guilt drive. It is very difficult for us to imagine that we are effective (or that our jobs are safe) if we have "nothing" to do.

Of course, while some people have a paranoid concern about being busy, other people truly understand that if they are to be effective as managers, they will continuously be engaging in managerial functions. That means that, however it may seem, they really won't have periods with nothing to do. Actually, it is usually the "doer" who may have periods with nothing to do, through working himself or herself out of a job. Good supervisors *never* seem to attain this point, because there is always *something* to do—planning the next operation or evaluating the last one. Thus the supervisor who fears that assigning work to a subordinate will leave him or her with nothing to do when the boss comes around is really making self-excuses demonstrating his or her own insecurity as a manager.

Unwillingness to Give Up Activities

Some supervisors fail to delegate work not because they feel guilty if they have nothing to do but because they are unwilling to give up certain activities which they personally enjoy doing. Psychologists have long since proven that it gives one a very satisfying feeling of accomplishment to be able to look at work completed and say "I did that." A chief executive who likes to forage around in the file cabinets, the director of marketing who likes to look up delivery schedules, the director of training who insists on teaching certain classes himself or herself are all examples of this attitude. This is an especially acute problem at the direct-supervision level because the supervisor has, in most cases, risen from the ranks and finds those activities which gave him or her the greatest feeling of accomplishment are not appropriate to a supervisor. Unless these people can get that rewarding feeling from overseeing *others* doing a job well (not unlike a coach getting vicarious pleasure from seeing his or her team win) then they will never be motivated to go on to higher levels of management.

When a supervisor can't enjoy seeing others "do" things, they also may not be able to make effective work assignments. Invariably, they will spend time usurping the duties of subordinates who should be doing the work. In fact, then, they do not make the "vital shift" discussed in Chapter 3, and so they begin to cheat themselves by coming to work early and staying late.

Impatience

Some line supervisors fail to delegate authority because of their own impatience. Many people, particularly those who are effective at accomplishing things, have an enormous sense of urgency, a tremendous drive to *do* things. They want things done "yesterday, if not before." Such people tend to be poor delegators of work, often doing the work themselves in the belief that this is the best way to ensure that it gets done. Yet the *effective* supervisor realizes that the more qualified hands there are working on the project, the quicker it will be done. Assuming that materials and facilities are available, and that the job is not completely linear (i.e., where each step depends on the one before), then certainly three workers can do a given job faster than one.

A sense of urgency is considered to be one of the essential attributes for a successful boss in our society. But it should be recognized that there is a big difference between urgency and impatience: A sense of urgency means a real drive to get things done; impatience means unwillingness to accept the fact getting them done takes time.

WHY EMPLOYEES DON'T DO THE WORK DELEGATED TO THEM

As has been mentioned, a supervisor might know and practice all the proper techniques for delegating work and still find that the one to whom the job was delegated doesn't do it. Of course, some people occasionally just simply refuse to do an assigned job, but that's a morale or discipline problem, and is not what we're talking about here. What we are concerned with here is the individual who presumably is willing to do the job but, for one reason or another, doesn't get it done.

Many subordinates fail to shoulder the responsibilities assigned to them because of certain mental attitudes or psychological hang-ups. This is not to say that people will avoid doing the work delegated to them only for subconscious reasons (sometimes their reasons are quite conscious) but that they often fail to perform because of feelings they have about their boss, or their job, or their own abilities, or a number of other things. In the rest of this chapter we will examine some of the reasons why some of those people who accept assignments nevertheless fail to complete them.

It's Easier to Ask the Boss than Make a Decision

Some subordinates can't be bothered with making a decision about an assignment when the supervisor is available to ask instead. And then there are some subordinates who just can't seem to bring themselves to make decisions—perhaps because they fear the responsibility. Both types bombard the supervisor with questions about decisions they should make for themselves. The supervisor should handle both types of subordinate tactfully; the one who is just dodging decisions should be discouraged from doing so, and the one who is afraid to make decisions should be encouraged to do so. But neither should feel so rejected that they then make *all* decisions for themselves—including those that should be made by the supervisor—because that can allow errors of judgment to delay, or perhaps even ruin, the whole assignment. Proper handling requires that the supervisor be diplomatic and have a keen sense of just how much is enough. That is, the supervisor must know which decisions he or she should make and which should be expected of the subordinate, and should be able to make the distinction clear to the subordinates without discouraging them.

Some supervisors, on the other hand, *require* that subordinates bring all problems to them, and may actually get angry with a subordinate who does not. Whatever the supervisor's motives, this is bad practice. In the first place, to discuss a decision which the subordinate could have made right on the job wastes time for both the subordinate and the supervisor. In the second place, it encourages the subordinate to be dependent on the supervisor when it is much better for all concerned for the subordinate to be as independent as possible, and thereby relieve the supervisor of most nonmanagerial concerns.

Perhaps the best arrangement is a careful application of the open-door policy, in which the supervisor is available for questions that are necessary but discourages those that are not, with the responsibility for deciding which is which resting largely with the subordinate. It was while visiting as a consultant at a firm in the midwest that the author saw an amusing presentation of the open-door policy: On the door of a supervisor's office was a sign that read, "If you're too damn dumb to figure it out yourself, come on in." While this might seem like a put-down of the subordinate with a question, it was taken in good humor and accomplished its purpose: It eliminated most of the unnecessary questions while announcing that the supervisor was available if needed.

Fear of Criticism

Nobody likes to be criticized, but some types of criticism are easier to take than others. For example, psychological studies have shown that, given a choice, people would rather be criticized for being lazy than for being stupid. Laziness is relative, after all—out of any 100 hard-driving corporation presidents, one will be lazier than the rest—and it does *not* mean that the lazy person doesn't know how to do his or her job. Stupidity is relative too, of course, but it *does* imply that the individual isn't capable of handling the assigned work. And that, in turn threatens that person's job security. For many people, then, it's safer to be thought lazy. After all, if you don't try, you can't fail.

The supervisor whose subordinates don't do their jobs as they should, even when they have the necessary time, facilities, and knowledge, should examine how he or she relates to those subordinates when they do something wrong. Even if a subordinate does make a stupid mistake, at least he or she was trying to do the job—not taking the lazy way out. In discussing the error with the subordinate, the supervisor should indicate that he or she is aware of this fact, and not shower the subordinate with destructive criticism. Criticism can—and should always—be constructive.

Lack of Incentive

Even a thorough and dependable employee is not likely to regard extra work, beyond what his or her job normally calls for, with any interest unless he or she has some incentive to do so. This is particularly true when the extra work occurs outside of regular working hours, but it applies during working hours as well. Even during working hours, employees might have little incentive to, say, implement a program to reduce wastefulness and operating expenses because it would take extra effort and give them no direct benefit.

An employee is most likely to feel some incentive to make an extra effort if he or she knows it will be recognized and appreciated—and the most concrete form of recognition can be shown when salary revue time comes around or promotions open up. On a day-to-day basis it helps for the supervisor to express verbally his or her appreciation for extra efforts made. Certainly the material rewards of an advance in position and/or salary can have great results, but for an employee to be told, "Thanks, that really helped," can also have a positive effect on morale and the incentive to make the little extra efforts that may be called for now and then.

Some Feel that Certain Work is Beneath Them

Some people suffer from delusions of grandeur; they genuinely feel that they were born of a privileged class and really don't have to do certain kinds of work. Some other people, who do not have such delusions, nevertheless feel that they are too good for some types of work. Still other people suffer from the notion that they don't have to do certain work because someone else ought to, or because it is beneath their dignity. We see these attitudes often both in the home and in certain caste situations at work. In the one case it's, "That's women's work," or "That's a man's job." In the other case it's, "That's apprentice work," or "The janitor is supposed to do that," or "Why don't we get *somebody* in here to clean this place up?"

There are many obvious examples of people refusing to do things because they feel it is not in their job description or that it is really somebody else's work to do. Practically always the work refused is "dirty work," and the people refusing it offer illogical reasons for their refusal.

Sometimes the refusal to do certain work is based on bigotry. Sometimes people will openly state that the work should be done by others whom the one refusing usually considers inferior—such as members of the opposite sex, different ethnic groups, or other social classes. Occasionally, too, they will argue that it is work for younger people (or older, depending on their own age.)

The feeling that "Rank has its privileges" also enables one to reject some types of work. The supervisor can pull that one, of course. And others can use it to argue that they've worked in the organization "so long" or "devoted so much attention" or "put in their time" and thus have earned certain privileges which excuse them from having to do some types of work. This is a two-edged tool, though. It can be used to boot an unwanted job *up* to those who claim privilege; "That's too important; the boss really ought to handle that one," or "The older people in the office have had the experience with that stuff. Give it to one of them."

Sometimes, of course, ideas about being privileged are deliberately built into the work relationship. For example, in union circumstances, seniority is a very real thing. In other situations, so is the key to the executive wash room or the name on the door or the assigned parking space. These conditions occur as the result of deliberate morale-building efforts by organizations and institutions. But privileges must not be abused, lest they become demoralizing to those who don't have them.

Some Figure the Boss will Change it Anyway

Some bosses are perfectionists; they insist that the job be done perfectly. Unfortunately, "perfect" often means different things to different people. And even where there are objective standards of perfection, we have already made the point that perfection may be unnecessary.

A perfectionist boss is very inclined to change or alter the work which the subordinate has done. This may very well irritate the subordinate, especially one who takes pride in the way he or she does things, who may not see any particular value or merit in the way the boss changes it. This is especially true where the boss obviously believes that his or her way is better than the subordinate's way; sometimes the boss simply won't let the employee do the job the way he or she wants to. And sometimes the results can be disastrous, as when, for example, the customer prefers the subordinate's methods to those of the boss, or when the employee builds up such feelings of resentment toward the boss that he or she deliberately does less or poorer work—or files a grievance or quits. There are many ways a resentful employee can act negatively if he or she chooses to.

What is the moral of the above story? Certainly perfectionism is important—*if* it's required. We want the pilot to have an equal number of takeoffs and landings; we want the surgeon to remove our appendix rather than our heart. However, in most situations there is practically always some degree of leeway available in the way any particular job is performed. The boss who is unnecessarily perfectionist or otherwise unduly demanding in having things done his or her way will probably succeed only in discouraging subordinates from shouldering responsibility.

Some are Privileged Characters

Sometimes people will avoid accepting work because they feel somehow, someway they are "privileged" and don't have to do certain things. The problem of the privileged-character employee is different from that of the individual who feels that certain work is beneath him or her. The privileged character feels somehow, someway, that he or she has special rights to do (or not to do) some things. The most common examples are those employees who have been with the organization for many years and so knew the owner—or somebody very close to the top—when he or she was "just one of us."

Actually, the privileged characters don't exist too often, but when they do they're maddening to their immediate superiors. It is virtually impossible for the direct supervisor to insist on optimum job performance from a privileged character; the supervisor knows that the privileged character can simply refuse to do things and will go to the "big boss" if the supervisor pressures him or her to perform.

It should be recognized that the big boss who responds to the privileged character's complaints fails to meet his or her responsibilities. At the least, this can cripple the direct supervisor's effectiveness; what's worse, it can destroy departmental morale. Nevertheless, we can occasionally see an unwise boss who actually encourages his or her friends to seek special privileges.

Lack of Pain Cost

Positive reinforcement is a very real thing. Psychologists, however, argue about the merits and demerits of punishment. Because there is some question about whether punishment is effective in getting people to do things, it will be suggested here that, even though it might be bad to punish, *lack* of punishment may be a contributing reason why people refuse to do things. Strange as it may seem, many subordinates fail to shoulder responsibility simply because there is very little that will be done to them if they don't do the job.

It is one thing to be motivated, and it's something else to be pushed. Some people will not do things because they are not motivated to do them, but they will do things if they are prodded. But when an employee simply doesn't want to do something, and feels that nothing will happen to him or her for not doing it, then the supervisor may be facing a problem of lack-of-pain cost. That is, the punishment for *not* doing a job is not enough to motivate the person to *do* it. The contingency theory of leadership, discussed in Chapter 4, indicates that the supervisor should go ahead and prod the people showing such an attitude not only with threats of punishment, but perhaps with very real actions. Until psychologists come up with a better solution, the reality of punishment may be the only thing that will motivate some people—at least at some times.

This chapter discussed many of the psychological and other problems that cause line supervisors to be ineffective at delegating work to subordinates. To some degree, these same problems exist for supervisors of supervisors and managers of managers. Some of them are unique to the line supervisor, however, because the line supervisor is practically always a "grownup doer" and has been promoted from a rank-and-file job. This often makes it difficult for the line supervisor to get his or her immediate subordinates to work as they should. Any astute line supervisor should check carefully to see whether he or she is having any of the problems discussed here.

EXERCISES

Of these eight activities, which are managing and which are doing jobs?*

	Doing	Managing
1. Deciding whether to add a position.	☐	☐
2. Approving a request from one of your people for a routine expenditure.	☐	☐
3. Reviewing monthly reports to determine progress toward achieving specific objectives for your area of responsibility.	☐	☐
4. Deciding what the cost budget shall be for your area of responsibility.	☐	☐
5. Interviewing a prospective employee referred to you by a friend.	☐	☐
6. Attending an industry conference to learn the latest technical developments.	☐	☐
7. Explaining to one of your people why he or she is receiving a raise.	☐	☐
8. Asking one of your people what they think about an idea you have for their area of responsibility.	☐	☐

Now check your answers against these explanations.

1. *Managing.* This is developing the organization structure.
2. *Doing.* Since the expenditure is a routine one, the executive should probably delegate this function and arrange for a periodic audit to be sure that correct procedures are followed.
3. *Managing.* This is measuring and evaluating.
4. *Managing.* This is planning and developing a budget.
5. *Doing.* This is performing a personal function, even though it's undoubtedly the considerate thing to do. Deciding to hire someone after all the recruiting and selecting has been done, however, would be staffing, a managing activity.

---

* Adapted from Raymond O. Loen, "Manager or Doer: A Test for Top Executives," *Business Management,* May 1966.

6. *Doing.* Since the stated intent is to learn the latest *technical* developments, it it questionable whether this will help the supervisor increase the results he or she gets through others.
7. *Managing.* This is motivating.
8. *Managing.* This is communicating, probably in order to develop a program. It could be a form of motivating if the purpose is to get participation now in order to get acceptance later.

Work through the following questions about how you do your job. Discuss your answers with others in your study group.

	Yes	No
1. Do you have to take work home almost every night?	☐	☐

If so, why?

Actions you can take to cut this down:

2. Do you work longer hours than those you supervise or than is usual for hourly paid workers in the business?	☐	☐

If "yes," steps you could take to change this to a "no" answer:

	Yes	No
3. Do you have little time for appointments, recreation, study, civic work, etc.?	☐	☐

Time could be obtained by:

4. Do you need two or more telephones to keep up with the job?	☐	☐

How did this come about?

Plans for doing something about it:

5. Are you frequently interrupted because others come to you with questions or for advice or decisions?	☐	☐

Why does this happen?

	Yes	No
Strategies for cutting down these interruptions:		
6. Do your employees feel they should not make work decisions themselves, but should bring all problems to you?	☐	☐

Examples:

To change this situation you could:

7. Do you spend some of your working time doing things for others which they could do for themselves?	☐	☐

Examples:

	Yes	No
Actions you might take to avoid this:		
8. Do you have unfinished jobs accumulating, or difficulty meeting deadlines?	☐	☐

Examples:

The jobs could be finished on time by:

9. Do you spend more of your time working on details than on planning and supervising?	☐	☐

If so, why?

For a better balance you could:

	Yes	No
10. Do you feel you must keep close tabs on the details if someone is to do a job right?	☐	☐

Examples:

11. Do you work at details because you enjoy them although someone else could do them well enough?	☐	☐

Examples:

What to do about this:

12. Are you inclined to keep a finger on everything that is going on?	☐	☐

Examples:

Yes No

Procedures to try instead:

13. Do you lack confidence in your workers' abilities so that you are afraid to risk letting them take over more details? ☐ ☐

Examples:

How you might break out of this pattern:

14. Are you too conscientious (a perfectionist) with details that are not important for the main objectives of your position? ☐ ☐

Examples:

New plans to try for this:

	Yes	No
15. Do you keep job details secret from workers, so one of them will not be able to displace you?	☐	☐

Examples:

New plans for action:

16. Do you believe that no supervisor should be rushed in order to justify his or her salary?	☐	☐

Why or why not?

A supervisor's principal job is:

17. Do you hesitate to admit that you need help to keep on top of your job?	☐	☐

Examples of help you could use:

	Yes	No
List subordinates who could be trained to give this help:		
18. Do you neglect to ask workers for their ideas about problems that arise in their work?	☐	☐

Examples:

To change this you could:

DELEGATION: MIDDLE MANAGEMENT'S EFFICIENCY INDICATOR

Middle managers, or superviors of supervisors, have many of the same problems of delegation that direct, or line, supervisors do—problems that can be dealt with much as the direct supervisor would deal with them. However, the middle manager's job is significantly different from the line supervisor's in that he or she is supervising supervisors, not doers. It is not surprising, then, that *some* of the problems encountered by the supervisor of supervisors are much different from those of the line supervisor, and must be dealt with differently. In this chapter and the next we will discuss those problems of delegation which exist not for the line supervisor, but for the supervisor of supervisors.

DECIDING WHAT TO DELEGATE

An article which appeared in *Industry Week* magazine a few years ago, entitled, "Toughest Job of All—Delegating," made the point that "the other side of delegation is passing the buck." Usually, middle levels of management are more sensitive to accusations of buck-passing than to deficiencies in delegation. It should be the other way around.

One of the really significant responsibilities of the middle manager is to know *what* work he or she is expected to do and *what* work he or she can delegate to a subordinate. Nathaniel Stewart conducted a study a few years ago in which he listed the ten dominant reasons given for "not delegating more":

1. My subordinates lack the experience.
2. It takes more time to explain than to do the job myself.
3. A mistake by a subordinate could be costly.
4. My position enables me to get quicker action.
5. There are some things which I shouldn't delegate to anyone.
6. My subordinates are specialists and they lack the overall knowledge that many decisions require.
7. My people are already too busy.
8. My subordinates just aren't ready to accept more responsibility.

9. I'm concerned about lack of control over my subordinate's performance when I delegate something to him or her.
10. I like keeping busy and making my own decisions.

Of these ten items *only* number five, which states that there are some things a manager simply should not delegate to anyone else, is valid; *all* the other items are alibies for not delegating more work.

The position of the middle manager is unique. Usually promoted from the ranks of the doers, he or she is not a chief executive who generally feels comfortable in delegating "doing" functions. Yet this person must try to perform like a chief executive—particularly if he or she has any desire to get to the top. Because of hesitancy to delegate responsibility, many supervisors of supervisors have difficulty in making the vital shift in management (discussed in Chapter 3). In the author's opinion, it has been proven time and again that the supervisors of supervisors who have the most and greatest problems are those who should be delegating more *and don't know it.*

As was pointed out in Chapter 3 (and illustrated in Fig. 5), middle managers—or supervisors of supervisors—should spend the greater part of their working time on management activities. Ideally, in fact, they should spend all their time managing, delegating all "doing" jobs to subordinates. However, there are some things that supervisors of supervisors cannot delegate: performance appraisals and reviews, for example; some planning activities and coordination; morale problems, of course, and coaching and developmental work; and, obviously, many assignments of confidential nature, as well as anything that has been delegated for them to do personally. But wherever supervisors of supervisors *can* delegate, they *should* delegate.

Delegation at the middle-management level is vital partly because it is the middle manager who bears the greatest responsibility for performance. Certainly the direct supervisor has serious responsibilities, but they are relatively limited and are more closely connected to "doing" operations; certainly, too, the manager of managers has gravely serious responsibilities, but they are more concerned with policy-making and are a step further removed from actual production. But the middle manager, or supervisor of supervisors, must live with the wage/cost projections of the labor contract, for example, and make up budgets, all while seeing to it that the people subordinate to him or her keep their own subordinates producing the organization's goods and services at the necessary levels of quantity and quality. It is frequently the middle manager who has the greatest difficulty in making the vital shift in management discussed earlier, who works many extra hours a day and seven days a week, and who spreads himself or herself far too thin.

Part of the pressure on the supervisor of supervisors comes from his or her difficulty in making the vital shift; part comes from being in the middle, from being the one who interprets management's needs to labor and labor's needs to management; and part from competition. Unless the middle manager is more or less satisfied with his or her position, he or she probably wants to rise further in the organization. Since the higher one goes, the fewer positions there are, the supervisor of supervisors who wants to advance has got to beat the competition. This often means doing that little bit (or whole lot) extra to acquire visibility and please one's boss.

All these pressures on middle managers mean that they must use their time to the best advantage—and this means that they *must* delegate as much and as effectively as they can.

THE IMPORTANCE OF DECISION-MAKING IN DELEGATION

Students of what makes effective supervisors and managers often marvel at the records created by those who have been very effective at middle and upper management levels in an organization. For example, in visiting various organizations—both governmental and private—this author often observes that ambitious, young "go-getters" study very carefully the success styles and patterns of those they emulate in their organization. Invariably, people who are young and ambitious, who have recently risen to or expect to arrive at the supervisor-of-supervisors level, get interested in what *makes* successful supervisors of supervisors and managers of managers.

It is often argued by those in middle and upper levels of management that decision-making is more important than anything else. A prominent executive with a major American industry, who is also a close personal friend of the author, has commented on different occasions that the true key to his personal success has been in being decisive.

Just exactly what is the key to decisiveness? How does one make a decision? How does making a decision affect the delegation of work to one's subordinates? Can one be decisive and also be an effective delegator of work, or do decisiveness and delegation conflict? All of these are questions which need to be answered.

Bosses who are effective at delegating work to subordinates almost always seem to act in similar patterns—not because certain behavioral patterns are all that will get success, but because people tend to act the same way in the same circumstances. A powerful politician in a communist country and a powerful politician in a capitalist country can get similar results from people with similar techniques. Likewise, a skilled executive in a volunteer organization may well use the same tactics as a skilled executive in a private, profit-making organization to get the same results.

As we have stated, decisiveness in directing an organization seems to be one of the essential ingredients that most successful supervisors of supervisors and managers of managers employ. By decisiveness, we don't mean the ability to decide whether one wants a coffee or tea with lunch; we mean firmness in direction, commitment, and willingness to back up that commitment.

Most good supervisors of supervisors—especially if they have effectively handled the vital shift in management—know exactly what they want to delegate. So far as we are concerned in this book, what they delegate concerns four major areas:

1. Bona fide problems or issues which require exploration, study, and recommendations for decisions (the recommendations come from the subordinate, the decision is made by the delegator).
2. All activities which come within the scope of the subordinate's

job and his or her abilities (sometimes also things which stretch those job parameters and abilities slightly—and, sometimes, even quite a lot).

3. Tasks which challenge the talents of the subordinates who report to the supervisor of supervisors (especially toward the achievement of company goals and the needs of individuals to grow and develop their own talents).
4. Problems or activities which, if well handled by the subordinate, can conserve the boss' valuable time.

GROUND RULES FOR EFFECTIVE DELEGATION BY SUPERVISORS OF SUPERVISORS

Where Possible, Act, Don't React

Dr. George S. Odiorne, in *How Managers Make Things Happen*,* points out that "management means action, not reaction." Dr. Odiorne says that "one of the major complaints of the experts in management development is that too many executives are looking for a 'gimmick.' " Further, he quotes management expert James O. Rice, past president of the American Management Association, as saying, " 'It's an appealing idea for some managers to think that maybe there is a magic formula which they can apply, thereby solving their problems. . . . I've been in this business quite a few years, and if there is such a formula, I haven't seen it.' "

In order to delegate effectively, the supervisors of supervisors must know the difference between actually farming out work to the subordinate and looking for some magic solution. Good supervisors of supervisors, particularly those who grow to become excellent managers of managers, realize that what is required at their level is a sense of urgency and a deliberateness of work assignment; jobs must be clearly defined, and the people to whom they are assigned must be fully informed about them; the functions of responsibility, authority, and accountability must be clearly delineated. Good delegators at the supervisor-of-supervisors level

* Odiorne, George S., *How Managers Make Things Happen*, Englewood Cliffs, N.J.: Prentice-Hall, 1961.

move to meet the conditions of good delegation before their subordinates ask them to. In short, they act rather than react.

Identify Priority Items

Good supervisors of supervisors try very definitely to identify priority jobs, tasks, and activities. They do not "hunt and peck"; they decide what needs to be done and act on their decisions immediately. They farm out jobs and projects as they are brought to their attention, and not on the basis of reaction to the crises that arise when work hasn't been done. If immediate action is not possible, they schedule it for a definite future date or time.

Cope with Obstacles

One of the best ways to cope with obstacles is to make subordinates responsible for *total* job activities and tasks, rather than portions of jobs. The reason for this is that an individual who is responsible for a total activity is in a better position to cope with minor problems which come up. The benefits are three-fold: (1) Responsibility and continuity are better established, which means less chance for error or delay; (2) the subordinate becomes familiar with the whole job instead of just part of it, which enables him or her to assume more responsibility another time; (3) the supervisor of supervisors spends less time on minor problems, which leaves him or her more time for management.

Use Other People's Ideas

Supervisors of supervisors who are going to be successful usually experience a big breakthrough in their thinking: They recognize that nobody has a monopoly on brains.

Newly appointed supervisors of supervisors have gotten to their position *largely because they worked hard* and have been pretty smart. As a result of this success, they often become very opinionated and think that their ideas are the best. Of course, self confidence is a valuable commodity for any manager, but anyone so naive as to feel that they alone know how things should be done will find that they do not use their subordinates effectively. This attitude, of course, keeps them from being effective delegators because of their lack of confidence in their subordinate's capabilities.

Pay Attention to Work Patterns and Programs

Effective supervisors of supervisors pay a great deal of attention to the way work is done particularly in respect to the habit patterns and routines of individual employees. Invariably, good supervisors of supervisors are reorganizers of work as much as they are organizers. They look at established work patterns with a questioning eye to determine whether materials, activities, and work routines can be reorganized, reassigned, or otherwise improved to eliminate bottlenecks, or whether work-flow problems could be overcome if subordinate managers more effectively controlled their work.

Assume the Posture of Coach

Good supervisors of supervisors view themselves more as coaches building teams than as bosses. One of the real breakthroughs in the supervisor of supervisors' mental attitude is to realize that he or she is no longer just a player on the team—not even a playing manager—but a coach, and it is his or her obligation as coach to be sure that both the players and the playing managers (direct supervisors) get guidance and help toward the major projects and goals for which they are to be responsible.

Know How to Use Committees

Don't use committees to accomplish work unless there is some very real need for them. Don't use committees for trivial matters, or where very direct and clear-cut responsibility is required for performance and action, or where one person can do the job. However, committees are useful to help resolve morale and motivational type matters when those kinds of problems arise, as well as for policy-making. And remember that a good supervisor of supervisors will not use committees to make decisions which he or she *personally* should resolve.

Know How to Handle Corrective Discipline

It is essential that the good supervisor of supervisors know how to handle undesirable situations—particularly those that require the reprimand of a subordinate. If those matters are handled poorly, the results can be catastrophic. Therefore, especially when reprimanding a subordinate (who is a direct supervisor) good supervisors of supervisors apply corrective discipline only when they have *all* the facts, are in control of their own emotions, have obtained both sides of the story, and feel that they can cope with the problem effectively.

When supervisors of supervisors do cope with disciplinary problems, they should always do so very firmly and fairly. Also, they should never carry a grudge about something a subordinate has done wrong or poorly and which they have had to correct.

Avoid Meddling

Good supervisors of supervisors do not meddle in the activities they have delegated to their subordinates or for which they hold their subordinates responsible. They do not like to be put in the position of having to spy on subordinates and so they are inclined to trust people until they have been proven to be untrustworthy.

Experienced supervisors of supervisors make certain that the information they are getting about any work problem is valid. They do this by talking to each responsible subordinate, comparing one subordinate's unit with another and otherwise "doing their homework." Beyond that point, however, they don't tell people what they must do, or when or under what circumstances they must do it, unless it is obvious that a situation is getting hopelessly out of control.

Be Decisive

Another ground rule that many middle managers use in trying to be effective delegators is to be decisive. This does not mean to make snap judgments or ill-conceived decisions, but make decisions based on knowledge and understanding of familiar territory.

It must be understood that while they don't make snap judgments, they are not afraid to make decisions. Furthermore, once the supervisor of supervisors has made a decision—and/or made a subordinate responsible for something—he or she does not reverse that decision without a compelling reason. If it turns out to be a bad decision—no matter why—that justifies reversal. But the good middle manager makes very few bad decisions. We will say more about decision-making later in this chapter.

COMMON PATTERNS OF POOR DELEGATION

In trying to be effective delegators of work, supervisors of supervisors engage in many common behavioral patterns, a number of which simply *don't* amount to effective delegation. On the next few pages we will discuss some of the more *negative* of these behavioral patterns.

Non-delegation For the supervisor of supervisors to simply talk to a subordinate about the duties which he or she normally expects that subordinate to do is not delegation. Nor is it delegation when the supervisor of supervisors asks a subordinate to do a job (conduct a survey, gather information, or whatever) while keeping all the decision-making to himself or herself. And it is not delegation to ask a person to work on a problem, but then later ask someone else (perhaps even a group or committee) to participate in solving it or in reviewing what the first person has done about it.

Delegation doesn't mean just telling somebody to do something and then expecting them to do it. Rather, delegation means actually making full use of the talents of the people who are available and giving them operating room and power to make all the necessary decisions.

Doing Something, Even if it's Wrong Many supervisors of supervisors fail at delegating because they feel that activity is important for its own sake; they subscribe to the old military maxim, "Do something, even if it's wrong." The problem with delegating work on the basis of "let's just get something going" is that there is no goal orientation; doing the work would be a purposeless function. Obviously a boss isn't delegating when he or she is just asking for activity.

The Pointless Job Sometimes supervisors of supervisors get into difficulty because they assign incomplete or even pointless activities to subordinates. It is one thing for an individual to be responsible for a whole job; it is something else to be responsible for part of a job which is not clearly defined.

Supervisors of supervisors who want to avoid this problem tend to follow three functional guidelines: (1) they assign the total job to an individual, (2) they try to anticipate, at the time of delegation, what crises are likely to occur, and prepare the subordinate for the decisions that he or she may need to make in order to solve or prevent them, and (3) they assign work only to those individuals whom they know to be capable of doing the jobs as they should be done.

The only way to make item (3) work is to have subordinate supervisors (direct supervisors) who are able to assume responsibilitity and push a job through to completion. Insofar as conditions permit, good supervisors of supervisors pick their direct supervisors very carefully.

Failure to Resolve Problems Many supervisors of supervisors encounter difficulties because: (a) they fail to find the causes of problems and (b) they don't really seek the solution. Too often when they assign work to subordinate managers they are thinking only in terms of the *end results,* and not the means of achieving those results. This inattention to problem resolution can create difficulties for them and for their subordinates.

Holding Preconceived Notions about How Work Should be Done We're all familiar with some form of the old line: "Don't confuse me with facts, my mind is made up." Oftentimes poor supervisors of supervisors will give the subordinates to whom they assign work no choice as to how the work will be done, or indeed, what the final result will be. Obviously, telling someone to do something *your* way is not effective delegation of work; it is simply going through the motions.

It is an even greater failure of effective delegation when the subordinate supervisor, after spending a great deal of time and effort on the project, finds that the supervisor of supervisors already has resolved the issue. Such a discovery is completely frustrating, and a few repetitions can demoralize all of the responsible middle manager's subordinates.

Project Overkill Sometimes, in attempting to be extraordinarily good delegators of work, supervisors of supervisors will overkill in farming out a project or problem to subordinates. It is questionable whether there is any true delegation going on when the supervisor is too meticulous and thorough in laying out the job assignment. In such cases, the subordinate may well wonder whether there is anything for him or her to actually do on the "delegated" job. This problem becomes especially acute when it begins to affect morale and motivation of the subordinate receiving the work assignment. Nothing can be more stifling than to feel that one is being paid for a job that is already done. And it's even worse when the subordinate feels that not only has the job already been done, but that he or she is merely a rubber stamp who is supposed to recommend and either (a) get no credit for it or (b) take the blame if things go wrong.

Indecision Many supervisors of supervisors are indecisive about what to delegate to their subordinates and under what conditions. Indecision creates tension in anyone; an indecisive person practically always is extremely difficult to work with. Decisiveness, in and of itself, is not it's own reward, but it does have virtues.

Naturally, in any delegation of work, certain things must be decided: Is the job delegated? Is the delegation to stick? What happens if the work is not done, or is done poorly or incorrectly? All of these questions have to be answered before one can truly assess the quality of his or her decisiveness as a boss.

Nondelegators and Nondelegation

Most good supervisors of supervisors can—and are expected to—delegate work which fits into the categories just mentioned. However, many people don't know what is expected of them, or at least don't know how to make the proper work assignments. Sometimes this is because they don't fully understand or appreciate the capabilities of their subordinates, other times it's because they simply are not delegating types—they don't know how to delegate or they don't feel well or secure about it.

Chapter 7 discusses what goes wrong when supervisors of supervisors attempt to delegate work and also what happens when their subordinates somehow or other avoid the responsibility delegated to them. For the next few pages, however, let us consider just eight behavioral patterns or characteristics of middle managers who do *not* delegate effectually—who are, in effect, nondelegators. Unquestionably there are others, but these eight can help us determine whether we are decisive enough to effectively delegate work to subordinates.

1. Failure to keep subordinates informed about plans the manager has for the total operation. Supervisors of supervisors who are truly in managerial planning and control positions necessarily will frequently be making new plans upgrading activities for their operational units. If they fail (for whatever reason) to keep their subordinates aware of what's going on or what is going to happen they will find it extremely difficult to delegate work to subordinates. A subordinate has to be up to date on an operation before it (or part of it) can be delegated to him or her, and updating a subordinate all at once is often so difficult that some bosses tend to feel that it just isn't worth the bother; it simply takes too much time and effort on their part. Thus they lapse into a nondelegating type of behavioral pattern.

2. Failure to require, get, and/or use progress reports. Some supervisors of supervisors fail to require progress reports because they don't realize how useful they can be. Some fail to get the progress reports they have requested because: (a) they don't insist, or (b) they don't use the ones they do get—which causes subordinates to feel, understandably, that making progress reports is just a waste of time. And some middle managers just don't use the progress reports they get—for a number of reasons. Now, since any supervisor of supervisors must be well-informed on a project before he or she can delegate any of it—or work related to it—those who do not require, get, *and* use progress reports tend to become nondelegators or ineffective delegators.

3. Unwillingness to let subordinates supply their own ideas. There are supervisors of supervisors who are unwilling to let subordinates think for themselves, develop ideas, or, particularly, implement those ideas. Of course, the subordinates involved become demoralized. Furthermore, this may bring backlash from the subordinates, in that they might even go out of their way to deliberately frustrate the boss' "better" plan.

4. Tendency to "dump" projects. Many supervisors of supervisors fail to delegate effectively because they "dump" projects on their subordinates all at once instead of assigning responsibility gradually. It is very rare that an individual can suddenly assume responsibility for an enormous number of projects and still perform well; practically always people grow into certain jobs and gradually assume responsibility. There are notable exceptions, of course; probably the reader can think of people who have functioned admirably when a tremendous work load was thrust upon them. But it is better for a manager to develop subordinates gradually, and let them grow into shouldering responsibility. Nondelegator type managers, however, practically always assume a "sink or swim" posture and violate this operating principle. As a result, they seldom succeed.

5. Failure to give the subordinate credit for shouldering responsibility. Everybody has certain feelings of pride in the work that they do, and most people who feel that they are accomplishing something want some form of recognition for what they have done. Good delegators of work—particularly at the supervisor-of-supervisors level—recognize that their immediate subordinates (direct-line supervisors) particularly like to have some recognition for what they have done and enjoy developing a feeling of responsibility for the work which they have accomplished.

Good delegators tend to keep out of areas of responsibility which have been delegated to subordinates, permitting them to take full pride in their achievements. Nondelegator personalities, of course, do the opposite. They meddle in the subordinate's affairs and are very willing to offer (unasked for) suggestions, changes, or "improvements." This practice, of course, badly demoralizes the subordinates, who become increasingly reluctant to shoulder responsibility for any major activity, feeling they will not get credit for it anyway.

6. Inattention to project completion. Subordinates who are doing well with their projects would like to have their supervisors know it. Subordinates who are having difficulty with their projects need a little help and encouragement. Good supervisors of supervisors keep themselves informed on how their subordinates' projects are going, knowing that a little recognition here and a little help there are good for both the subordinates and the projects they are working on.

Showing interest, however, does not mean meddling; unnecessary interference is bad for morale. It is economically bad, as well, for it wastes the time of the manager either on "doing" activities or on management activities which need not have been done. A good supervisor of supervisors should be able to tell when his or her intervention is needed on a project and when it is not—and in the latter case should leave the project alone.

When a supervisor of supervisors forgets about a project, or just fakes an interest in it, the subordinate will know it, will assume that his or her project is not very important, and may slow down or become careless about the job. Interested attention to the completion of a project, then, is important—and failure to show it is another mark of the nondelegator type of manager.

7. Lack of respect for subordinates' ambitions. In most cases line supervisors aspire to become supervisors of supervisors. Consequently, they work hard at doing their job and doing it well. Even when they're not interested in promotion, they practically always want to do their job well simply as a matter of pride and for feelings of achievement.

Often line supervisors suggest ideas to their supervisors of supervisors. If the supervisor of supervisors shows disrespect for these ideas by ignoring them or ridiculing them, the line supervisor will be offended and may become less efficient even without meaning to. And he or she may even go so far as to deliberately hinder the functioning of the supervisor of supervisors. Thus contempt for the ideas of subordinates is typical of the nondelegator, not the good supervisor.

8. Failure to back up a subordinate when a decision is made. When delegated projects or assignments are going well, everything is fine; everybody is everybody's friend, people will back up each other, and so on. However, when things go *wrong,* oftentimes it causes a reversal to dog-eat-dog, uncivilized behavioral patterns.

Some individuals are very quick to drop the ball when it comes to backing up their subordinates. They don't want to look bad themselves, and feel that if they back up a subordinate who looks bad, or approve what he or she did, then they look bad too. The fallacy of this thought process is obvious. There is a decided difference between spinelessness and poor judgment. No one expects a boss to back up a subordinate who has done something genuinely stupid. However, when the subordinate has acted logically on the basis of the knowledge available at the time the decision was made, and when the supervisor of supervisors has backed up the subordinate in the implementation of that decision, then for the supervisor to fail to back up the subordinate when the chips are down is unpardonable in anyone's eyes—including those of the big boss. Yet many nondelegator type people are, at best, badly lacking in loyalty when their subordinates are in trouble.

EXERCISES

1. In a poll of several hundred executives from a cross-section of business and industrial firms the following were some of the dominant reasons given for "not delegating more." Indicate which reasons you feel are valid by checking the box under the **V**, which ones you consider an alibi by checking the **A**, and the ones you consider questionable by checking **?**.

	V	**A**	**?**
a) My subordinates lack the experience.	☐	☐	☐
b) It takes more time to explain than to do the job myself.	☐	☐	☐
c) A mistake by a subordinate can be costly.	☐	☐	☐
d) My position enables me to get quicker action.	☐	☐	☐
e) There are some things I shouldn't delegate to anyone.	☐	☐	☐
f) My subordinates are specialists and they lack the overall knowledge that many decisions require.	☐	☐	☐
g) My people are already too busy.	☐	☐	☐
h) My subordinates just aren't ready to accept more responsibility.	☐	☐	☐

	V	A	?
i) I'm concerned about lack of control over the subordinate's performance when I delegate something to him or her.	☐	☐	☐
j) I like keeping busy and making my own decisions.	☐	☐	☐

2. Discuss your answers to the above test with your study group.

3. Of those factors in Exercise 1 which you concluded were essentially alibis, discuss with your group how these can best be overcome if they continue to be obstacles to delegation. Define what measures you would recommend be taken to alleviate these obstacles by the delegator. By the subordinate. By the company or institution you work for.

4. Outline your delegation preparedness by answering the following questions:
   a) Do you and your subordinates agree on what results are expected of them? *Yes — No —*
   b) Do you and your subordinates agree on measures of performance? *Yes — No —*
   c) Do your subordinates feel that they have sufficient authority over personnel? *Yes — No —*
   d) Do your subordinates feel that they have sufficient authority concerning finances, facilities, and other resources? *Yes — No —*
   e) Within the past six months what additional authority have you delegated to them?

   f) What more does each of your subordinates think should be delegated to them?

g) Is accountability fixed for each of your delegated responsibilities? *Yes* — *No* —
Is your follow-up adequate? *Yes* — *No* —

h) Are you accessible when your subordinates need to see you? *Yes* — *No* —

i) Do your subordinates fail to seek or accept additional responsibility? *Yes* — *No* —

j) Do you bypass your subordinates by making decisions which are part of their job? *Yes* — *No* —

k) What interferes with the effective use of your management team?

l) Do you do things your subordinates should do? *Yes* — *No* — Why?

m) How could you best improve your delegation?

n) If you were incapacitated for six months, who would take your place?

o) Ask each of your subordinates individually: "What could I do, refrain from doing, or do differently which would help you do a better job?"

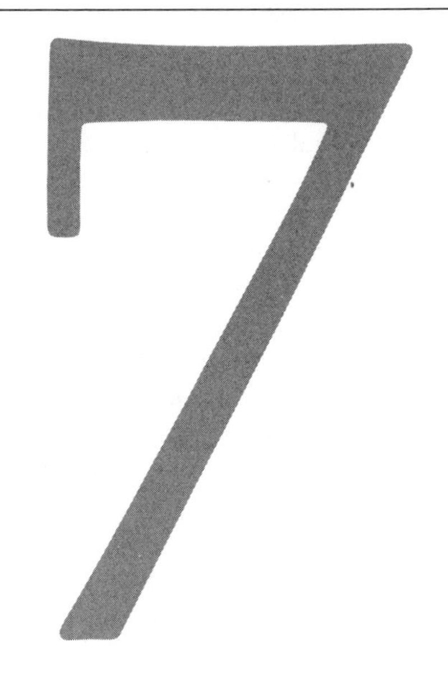

DELEGATION VS. RELEGATION: MIDDLE MANAGERS' GRIEF

Several decades ago a well known management expert wrote an article describing the peculiar problems of delegation faced by supervisors of supervisors. He stated that supervisors of supervisors find their positions in their organization circumscribed by very definite constraints; they can offer recommendatons, but cannot *make* organizational policy; they can participate in organizational objectives, but cannot determine them. Planning and control is within the purview of the supervisor of supervisors not in a directorial sense, but only in an integrative sense. Supervisors of supervisors must see to it that working people are motivated to work, yet there is little they can do to provide motivation because they are removed from direct daily contact with the working part of the organization; their job is to lead.

New supervisors of supervisors have a great adjustment to make. When they were direct supervisors they rarely examined what it was that made them successful in that job; they usually just reacted on an intuitive, gut-level basis. Their instincts were sound, and that probably contributed to their promotion, but for supervisors of supervisors, instinct will not be enough—they will have to be able to recognize and evaluate what they do that works, why they do it, and why it works, and they must be equally analytical about what doesn't work. They may also find that the behaviors, talents, and skills that made them good line supervisors are not quite what they need to be good supervisors of supervisors—and even less what they need to become, eventually, good managers of managers. This need to modify one's behaviors, talents, and skills to suit the level of management is a continuing phenomenon of promotion, and becomes increasingly important as the span of control broadens and the organizational heirarchy deepens to encompass more and more operational units and personnel.

So far as delegation is concerned, one of the most important things that the supervisor of supervisors must recognize is that delegation at the middle-management level does not mean simply farming out the job and telling someone what to do. It is more a matter of assigning whole ideas, projects, or areas of responsibility to subordinates who, in turn, subdivide the various functional, mechanical, and operative procedures among responsible individuals. The single biggest problem of the new supervisor of supervisors is to understand just how to go about effectively delegating whole functions and/or projects to subordinates. Sometimes projects don't get done because of the psychological or behavioral limitations of the supervisor of supervisors; sometimes they don't get done because of what the subordinates get away with (or without).

DIFFICULTIES WITH DELEGATION

The problems encountered by a supervisor of supervisors in trying to be an effective delegator of work are not necessarily (and certainly not always) the result of his or her own psychological or behavioral limitations. Sometimes organization policies or procedures aggravate—or even create—problems. Other times, of course, the same could be said of the employees being supervised. However, the bulk of the middle manager's problems are not deliberately raised (consciously or otherwise) by either the organization or subordinates; they are more likely to be problems that "go with the territory." We will examine some of these in the next few pages.

Problems of "The Code"

People who become supervisors of supervisors want very much to be successful. They have a good idea of what that requires; they understand that their job is to manage, not to "do," and they try hard to assume the proper role. This is not difficult for those who have always worked at some managerial level—who may have gone into managerial work directly from school—but it *is* difficult for those who started out in the rank and file and then moved up. The latter, unfortunately, often have trouble with "The Code."

We mentioned "The Code" briefly in Chapter 5, when we discussed some of the reasons why supervisors fail to delegate—specifically, "I can do it better myself." But in addition to that claim, "The Code" also states, "Don't ask anyone else to do what you can't do yourself." Observing "The Code" can be very important to the middle manager who has come up from the rank and file; it is the most effective way of maintaining status among the doers, with whom the manager still identifies. The supervisor of supervisors remembers very well the common feeling of the doer whose work has been criticized—"I'd like to see that S.O.B. do it any better himself (herself)"—and wants to be sure that it can't be said of him. And of course there's the old feeling that you can't really boss a job until you've done it yourself.

Well, none of these attitudes is valid; in fact, they're not even logical. Except for those who specialize in such things, how many of us tune our own car—or piano? And even a dentist, who is certainly a specialist, gets his or her teeth cleaned by someone else. No, the only reason for a supervisor of supervisors to observe "The Code" is to gratify his or her ego. A middle manager is at the last level at which he or she can be considered a doer to any degree, and while "doing" work may be reassuring, he or she should engage in it *only* when it is essential—and that should be very rarely.

Uncertainty about Objectives

Like the direct supervisor who sometimes cannot decide what part of a job to assign to which worker, the supervisor of supervisors may have times when he or she is not sure just what his or her performance goals or objectives are. However, the difference is that the supervisor of supervisors must define performance objectives in terms of *total* projects rather than as pieces of projects. At this stage it is important for the middle manager to see the end product as it relates to total production or output or results, and not as partial production. For example, it is one thing for a pilot to make an emergency landing at a busy airport, but it is something else entirely for the flight controller in the tower to integrate that pilot's plane with numerous other aircraft waiting to land or take off, with fire trucks, ground crew, and ambulances—all to achieve maximum safety to the aircraft in question with minimum interruption of the airport's normal functions.

The one requirement common to all supervisors of supervisors is that they *must* be able to determine just how acceptably their unit is progressing toward the goals or objectives of the organization. Delegating work to a subordinate requires that the boss understand what his or her organization unit has to accomplish. One reason why so many organizations in the United States have developed middle management training programs around the idea of Management By Objectives* is that people do not always understand what their role as supervisor of supervisors is. According to Richard J. Nachman, a prominent authority on executive development programs, one of the biggest problems encountered in developmental programs designed for those at the supervisor-of-supervisors level is to help them determine how to set total project goals and performance objectives for their organizational unit. It's not that the individual is reluctant to set performance goals or objectives, but that he or she is unable to define the results expected from them. And the middle manager who does not see these performance indicators clearly is going to have difficulty delegating to subordinates those areas of responsibility which, when completed, will support the accomplishment of the total organizational goals and objectives.

Judgmental Problems

Some supervisors of supervisors have difficulty in being objective about the competence or capability of their subordinates, the direct supervisors.

People who get promoted to be supervisors of supervisors inevitably are very competent people; further, they are practically always highly self reliant. Such people may find it difficult to trust the judgment of their subordinates. Part of the problem is that they want things to be done their way and they are not sure that the subordinate will achieve an output that truly is acceptable to them. Other times, of course, they simply lack confidence in the individual's capability to perform. If the middle manager has already been disappointed by the subordinate's performance, then his or her caution may be justified. Otherwise, however, failure of the supervisor of supervisors to objectively evaluate the capabilities of subordinates can only hamper his or her own performance as a middle manager.

---

* According to a study made in 1972 by the University of Utah College of Business Administration, 55 percent of the Fortune 500 companies use formal MBO programs.

Lack of Feedback

Another reason why many supervisors of supervisors fail at delegating work to their subordinates is that they do not set up a feedback or control mechanism which will assure that the job is being done. Good supervisors of supervisors, of course, know that they can exert two kinds of managerial control: *preventive,* which consists of procedures or standards designed to be implemented *before* errors or mistakes occur; and *corrective,* which consists of actions designed to correct mistakes *after* they've occurred.

The lower organizational levels, especially the line supervisors, practically always use corrective control. After all, the line supervisor is practically always on the job and can take immediate corrective action when things go wrong. Very little time or effort need be devoted to setting up preventive controls. In fact, if preventive controls are set up, it is usually at the instigation of the supervisor of supervisors or manager of managers in charge of the unit (or as a result of problems anticipated by Engineering or Quality Assurance people).

The supervisor of supervisors, however, is not so immediately aware of problems, which can sometimes get beyond control before corrective measures can be taken. Because of this time lag, preventive control is far more valuable than corrective control to the middle manager.

Unfortunately, supervisors of supervisors, particularly those who are new on the job, are seldom prepared to develop preventive controls. Most of them, as we have said, have come up from the rank and file, and their training and development up to the time of their promotions largely consisted of "fire-fighting" tactics, or corrective control. But until the supervisor of supervisors can develop effective preventive control mechanisms which will enable him or her to know that things at the direct-supervision and "doing" levels are going well, he or she will be reluctant to delegate responsibility to subordinates.

Inability to Operate in the Face of Uncertainty

Rich man, poor man, beggar man, thief—all of us act differently in those areas in which we know our way around than we do in areas that are strange to us. On familiar ground we act with confidence;

on strange ground, most of us do not. The middle manager who has confidence in his or her subordinates will delegate to them; the one who doesn't, won't. Of course, some people do handle ambiguous situations with some degree of confidence. To illustrate, look at Fig. 10; from it, pick out the symbol that is different from all the others.

Did you pick the circle? You're right; it's the only one that has no corners. Did you pick the small square? You're right; it's the only one that is much smaller than the others. Did you pick the rectangle? You're right; it's the only one whose height does not equal its width. Or did you reply that the question of which symbol is different from the others is not valid without further definition? You're right about that, too; you really should have more information. The point is, then, that there may be no *single* right answer.

Some people handle this sort of ambiguity better than others, and it is a skill that can be acquired through practice. The capable supervisor of supervisors should train himself or herself to be quite good at it, because it can have a great influence on how well he or she succeeds as a middle manager. The *direct* supervisor can always check up on how an assignment is going, if he or she thinks it necessary. This is not so easy at the middle-management level, however, (and even less so at higher levels), so the supervisor of supervisors should develop the habit of acquiring enough information to permit selection of the best "right" answer available at the time.

Distrust of Subordinates

Not many people would admit to being distrustful, but many would feel free to acknowledge "a healthy skepticism" about this, that, or the other thing. But even a healthy skepticism can be a handicap to a supervisor of supervisors, particularly one who is relatively insecure and lacks confidence about his or her ability to do the job. For such a person, skepticism can easily become distrust.

Whatever the reason for the distrust—belief that the subordinate doesn't understand how to do the job, or doesn't appreciate its critical importance, or even doesn't *want* to do it right—the super-

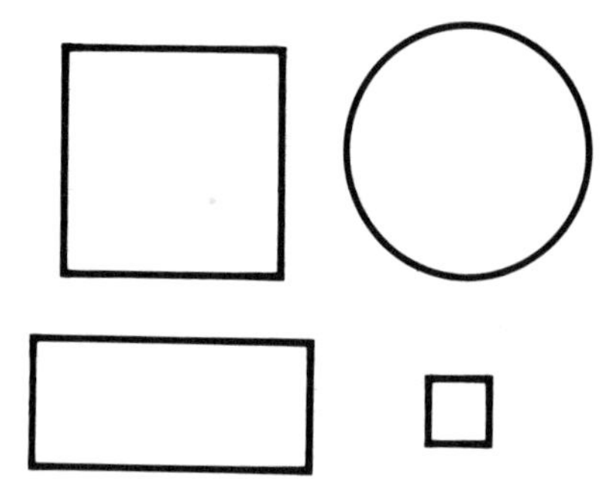

Figure 10

visor of supervisors should do whatever is necessary to get rid of the feeling. No supervisor can function with the necessary effectiveness unless he or she can delegate work to subordinates with some degree of confidence.

Competitiveness with Subordinates

Not unlike distrust of subordinates—and frequently a companion of distrust—is the feeling of competitiveness which some supervisors of supervisors feel toward their subordinates. Most supervisors of supervisors are quite pleased and proud to have gotten where they are in their careers. Unfortunately, however, some are also fearful that a subordinate will get their job (or show up better than they at some time).

Because of this fear, many supervisors of supervisors are reluctant to assign jobs to subordinates at which the subordinates have shown outstanding ability. Instead, they keep these subordinates obscure by assigning them only jobs of relatively minor importance, jobs from which the subordinates are not likely to acquire any high visibility or recognition.

Competitiveness is seldom a problem with direct supervisors. Because of the mechanical nature of the work at the doer level, the direct supervisor is usually happy to delegate work to a subordinate who can do it better than he or she can. (Exceptions to this do occur. See Chapter 5.) At the supervisor-of-supervisors level, however, the work is more intellectual than mechanical, and it becomes difficult to prove one's worth in terms of production or units of output. Then an ego problem emerges, most commonly in the form of competition for recognition as to who has actually done a good job. This drive for identification will often cause a supervisor of supervisors to be selective in the work which he or she delegates. Specifically the supervisor of supervisors may save the good jobs for himself or herself, and give the less desirable jobs to the subordinate. Naturally, the subordinates resent this, particularly if they, too, are ambitious and would seriously like to do something of merit to gain recognition.

Unfortunately, supervisors of supervisors do not always recognize the fact that such conduct limits their own capacities as supervisors and reduces their unit's productiveness. And this, in turn, reflects poorly on their administrative ability. Competitiveness with subordinates sometimes becomes chronic in executive suites, among managers of managers, and we will discuss this further in Chapter 9.

The Martyr Complex

We mentioned in an earlier chapter that some direct supervisors feel guilty if they don't have any "doing" work to take care of. To a certain extent this is also true about supervisors of supervisors. However, the latter have a problem in delegation which is totally unlike the guilt feelings of the direct supervisor. That is the *martyr complex,* which is a neurotic need of the subject to feel that he or she is overworked and underpaid. The simplest, most direct way of satisfying this need is for the middle manager to retain and do jobs which should logically be delegated to a subordinate.

While the martyr complex can sometimes be found among direct supervisors and the rank and file, it is most common among supervisors of supervisors. Part of the reason for this is that those supervisors of supervisors who have not genuinely made the vital shift in management tend to work longer hours than do their subordinates or superiors. Consequently, playing the role of the really hard worker—the martyr—is good form in many people's eyes.

We are not talking now about the extra-time game that is played in so many corporations, in which managers of a certain level and above are expected to come in early and to stay late and/or work an occasional (or frequent) Saturday. In such organizations even good delegators play *that* game, because it can be disastrous for them not to. No, here we are talking about the individual who has a morbid psychological need to feel—and to show to others—that he or she is working harder, and putting in longer hours, than anyone else in the organization. Such a person is reassured of his or her own value and importance when he or she hears: "I don't know how you do it. You have the most fantastic capacity for work; you work harder than any other person I know. I don't know how this place would get along without you."

But supervisors of supervisors who take satisfaction or pleasure from such comments would do well to examine just how effectively they are performing their *managerial* roles. It is one thing to be genuinely "a damned hard worker," but it is unintelligent to carry that role to extremes. It is doubly unintelligent for a manager to spend extra time on "doing" activities, especially to the neglect of managerial functions. And it is triply unintelligent, not to say stupid, to do so knowingly!

Fear of Criticism

Some supervisors of supervisors fail to delegate work to subordinates out of fear of criticism. They are afraid that their subordinate will accuse them of having "dumb" ideas or ill-conceived plans—or even laugh at them behind their back. Some supervisors of supervisors will even do a job themselves rather than risk such reactions from the subordinates to whom they would normally assign it. This is just plain poor management, of course, for any individual who is a strong delegator of work must realize that, on occasion, he or she *must* make assignments which are not necessarily enjoyable or desirable, and which may not even seem logical. But subordinates are being paid to do the work assigned to them, and the supervisor of supervisors should not be reluctant to assign undesirable tasks any more than he or she should rejoice to assign desirable tasks.

RELEGATION OF WORK BACK TO THE BOSS

As was pointed out in earlier chapters, while bosses sometimes fail at delegating work to their subordinates because of their own inadequacies, other times they fail because the workers squirm out of shouldering responsibilities.

To some degree the middle manager's problem of getting subordinates to do work is similar to that of the direct supervisor. In other cases, however, they are decidedly dissimilar. For the rest of this chapter we will discuss some of the reasons why work assignments sometimes end up back on the desk of the supervisor of supervisors when he or she believes that they have been effectively delegated to a subordinate.

Subordinate's Need to Avoid Mistakes

Many people have a psychological need not to be wrong. Some people, in fact, have overwhelming drives to prove that they weren't wrong, *no matter what the outcome was*—as, for example, the individual who says, "I realize the report was put in six weeks late, and four weeks after the absolute cutoff point, but after all, *there weren't any mistakes* in what *I* did on it."

Usually the direct supervisor (the middle manager's subordinate) will not miss the deadline or simply refuse to do the job. More commonly he or she will work around the problem, churning ideas, but never making any definite moves until the boss gets impatient and starts pushing for the job to be done. Then the subordinate can take advantage of the opportunity to say, "Well, I suggested we could do (this or that), but you never said one way or the other." At that point, of course, the boss will say "Well, do this," and then the subordinate is off the hook; he or she has successfully returned to the boss the responsibility for ideas and decisions that was delegated to him or her in the first place. And since the boss made the decision, the subordinate has avoided any chance of being wrong.

Apple-polishing

Not everybody who tries to induce the boss to make decisions for them does so to avoid the risk of making a mistake. Some do it to make points. Consider: When a subordinate who should be qualified to make a decision instead asks the boss (in a duly solicitous fashion) what to do, then he or she is saying, in effect, "Oh Almighty who knows so much more than I, what guidance will you give me on this all-important subject?"

It is heady to any of us to be asked our opinions and advice, especially on a subject we presumably know something about. Obsequious subordinates cue in on this fact; they know it makes the boss feel good—*and* it also takes them off the hook in case the decision turns out bad or the project is spoiled for whatever reason. Thus bosses who are especially susceptible to this type of praise find the work they delegated returned to them.

Perceived Lack of Information

Subordinates who feel that they do not have enough information or knowledge to handle the job delegated to them usually feel that they have only two options: they can try to fake it, and run the risk of getting into really serious trouble, or they can take the job back to the supervisor of supervisors for help. Naturally, the best thing is to be honest and tell the boss they don't know how to handle the assignment. In most organizations, especially those that have an official open-door policy, the boss will be readily available to hear the subordinate's story and offer guidance toward a solution. Note that word "guidance." If the subordinate really does not know to handle the job, the best way for the supervisor to help is *not* to give him or her the necessary knowledge or information, but to help guide him or her to it. The supervisor of supervisors should *not* be involved in getting information for the subordinate, but only in teaching the subordinate how to get it.

Here the subordinate is in what several disciplines refer to as "a learning situation," and it has long been established that the things we learn for ourselves we understand better and retain longer than the things that are done for us. For the supervisor of supervisors to help the subordinate acquire the necessary information and knowledge for himself or herself is preferable for two reasons: It allows the subordinate to solve the problem in the way that is best for him or her (and for the organization, since the subordinate is being educated in the process), and it takes a minimum of time away from the middle manager's other managerial activities.

Too Much to Do

On some occasions a subordinate may avoid doing a delegated task because he or she already has too much to do. No matter how well organized an individual may be, there's a limit to how much he or she can do in a day, month, week, or year. That outside limit can't be surpassed for too long.

Presumably no supervisor of supervisors wants his or her subordinates to do more than they can possibly handle, but the fact is that probably most of us do not work to our fullest capacity all of the time, and maybe not even *most* of the time. Sometimes we may be like the old farmer who said to the young agricultural agent, "Sonny, you don't need to tell me all that stuff about efficiency, I'm not farming half as good now as I know how." We can probably all exert ourselves for that little bit of extra effort for an extra day, week, or month, but we are not talking about that type of extra exertion here. No, here we are talking about the problem of asking subordinates to do something when they *really* don't have enough time to do it; when they are already giving that extra something.

Well, what then? Does the supervisor of supervisors simply do the work himself or herself? No. When the unit's workload gets to the point where it can't all be done at once, then some things will simply have to wait. What the middle manager must do in that case is to organize work assignments and job delegations in order of priority, so that the most important things get done first, while less important things are permitted to wait until additional help or time is available. Of course top management should be informed of such action. If they can't get the middle manager the help he or she needs, then they will still need to know for purposes of their own planning.

Lack of Self-Confidence

A person who lacks self-confidence tends to avoid responsibility—especially when he or she has a low opinion of himself or herself. Of course, anybody can be less than confident at some time or other, but for some people that condition is chronic. Managers of managers rarely have to deal with this problem in themselves or in their subordinates; one rarely gets to middle management or higher without plenty of self-confidence (and some may have a bit more than their abilities justify). Supervisors of supervisors, however, do see this problem in their subordinates because direct supervisors oftentimes feel they are somehow not worthy of the jobs they have and aren't really sure they can shoulder additional responsibility.

Developing self-confidence in a subordinate is extremely difficult. Yet those who teach about the achievement motive argue that people's self-confidence can be developed by carefully assigning them work on an achievable basis, helping them to realize that they can do the job, and then helping them recognize the fact that they can do the whole job.

As was mentioned earlier, it is extremely important that the supervisor of supervisors gradually develop his or her subordinates to the point where they can assume greater responsibilities, rather than to simply dump whole projects on them. This gradual development is particularly important when the subordinate lacks self-confidence.

The Nonachievement Syndrome

So far as the job is concerned, the nonachievement syndrome essentially amounts to the death wish. Some people don't like to achieve, and others almost delight in failing (they're not the same thing). This syndrome is not directly related to ability—it can affect those who are highly capable as well as those who are not. It is a psychological problem, often serious, and its treatment is beyond the scope of this book. It is enough to say that there is little a supervisor can do about a subordinate's nonachievement syndrome from a functional standpoint. An individual so afflicted is best referred to a psychologist or psychiatrist for help.

Greed for High-Payoff Tasks

We mentioned in Chapter 5 that rank and file workers may sometimes try to get out of doing an assignment because it doesn't carry enough reward with it. This, of course, is a problem that the direct supervisor has to deal with. But the direct supervisors create a similar problem for supervisors of supervisors when they do essentially the same thing. The assignment the direct supervisor is trying to avoid may carry certain incentives with it, but the job he or she is trying to get may provide even greater incentives for its completion. Naturally, the direct supervisor will prefer to do the job with the highest payoff.

We see this circumstance commonly when a manager of managers is psychologically playing games with a supervisor of supervisors and his or her subordinate in turn. If the direct supervisor involved sees that the manager of managers is about to throw him or her a bone or otherwise play him or her off against the supervisor of supervisors, inevitably the direct supervisor will go after the higher payoff task of acceeding to the feelings and desires of the "big boss."

A situation in which the subordinate is going after a high payoff task, and thus avoiding less rewarding responsibilities, is not only a problem to supervisors of supervisors; it can be quite common to the manager of managers as well. The total dimensions which it may take are enormous—and, sometimes, vastly amusing. (More attention will be devoted to this subject as a problem of the manager of managers in a later chapter).

Lack of Agreement about Duties

The direct supervisor has very little trouble with this problem because the duties of his or her subordinates (the rank and file) are usually very clearly spelled out in job descriptions and/or union contracts. The supervisor of supervisors has more trouble with it, but still not much, because the jobs of his or her subordinates (the direct supervisors) are still of a relatively functional and mechanistic nature. The manager of managers, however, often has a great deal of trouble with this problem, because the duties of his or her subordinates (the supervisors of supervisors) may frequently include gray areas where responsibilities are not clearly spelled out—and even if they were, might possibly vary a bit with circumstances. (This problem of the manager of managers will receive more attention in Chapter 9.)

In this chapter we have assessed many of the reasons why many supervisors of supervisors fail at effectively delegating responsibility to their subordinates. We also explored many of the more common explanations of how and why their subordinates avoid shouldering responsibilities that the supervisors of supervisors would like to assign to them. In Chapter 8 we will begin to consider the problems of managers of managers.

EXERCISES

1. Discuss the difference between delegation and relegation. What do these differences mean in your organization? Give examples.
2. The author has described "The Code" as it affects (poor) delegation of supervisors of supervisors. Do you agree with "The Code?" Why or why not? How does it apply to managers in your organization?
3. What do you feel are the common reasons supervisors fail at delegating in your organization as a result of excessive competitiveness? How might these causes be overcome?
4. Is the martyr complex a real delegation hangup for anyone you know? If yes, do you ever behave in a like fashion? Does your company require long, hard hours of work? Is this productive? Reasonable?
5. How should you handle a request for information from a subordinate? Is this something to watch for in your job? Give examples.
6. What are the four biggest reasons you feel that employees in your organization relegate work up to supervisors of supervisors? How could this be cured?

POLICIES, DECISIONS, AND IMPLEMENTATION: THE EXECUTIVE'S PROBLEM

No less a man than Theodore Roosevelt once said, "The best executive is one who has enough sense to pick good men to do what he wants done, and self-restraint enough to keep from meddling with them while they do it."

Those who rise to high positions in large organizations know that every position should carry with it a specified set of tasks or responsibilities. Furthermore, it is generally acknowledged that this policy should be extended down to the lowest level in the organization at which there is sufficient competence, talent, and information. Unfortunately, this is not as easily done as said.

It is truistic to say that most executives or managers of managers realize the advantages to be found in effective delegation. Furthermore, the author's experience suggests that an overwhelming majority of executives will claim that they can *and are able* to delegate, that they do so relatively well, and, furthermore, that they do so freely.

Unfortunately, however, many lower-level managers, both direct supervisors and supervisors of supervisors, report that they feel they lack the authority they need to carry out the responsibilities that are assigned to them (and for which they are held accountable) by higher-echelon managers. If the subordinates do in fact have the necessary authority, then the manager of managers must consider two possibilities: Either the subordinates do not accurately perceive what the manager of managers is doing, or the manager of managers isn't doing what he or she thinks he or she is doing.

This chapter will address this fundamental difference between what the boss and the subordinate think the boss is saying and doing. We will not be trying to determine who is right and who is wrong, but simply to examine the problem and some possible solutions.

CONVERTING POLICY DECISIONS TO OPERATIONAL PLANS

In any organization it is a serious problem to convert policy level decisions made by chief operating executives into operational objectives for other people throughout the organization. To illustrate this point, George S. Odiorne, in his book *Management and the*

Activity Trap,* reports the following: Each of several chief executives was asked to list the major responsibilities of one of their own subordinates, and, for each area of responsibility identified, define the results expected from that subordinate. Then each of the subordinates concerned was asked to do the same for himself or herself —to identify his or her own areas of responsibility and the results he or she expected to produce. The degree of correlation between the executives' expectations of their subordinates and the subordinates' expectations of themselves was quite interesting:

- ☐ In respect to the subordinates' regular, recurring, and ongoing responsibilities, the average boss and subordinate failed to agree about 25 percent of the time.
- ☐ As a result of that failure to agree on regular responsibilities, disagreement on what major problems exist and should be solved ran to approximately 50 percent.
- ☐ Worst of all, disagreement between boss and subordinate about what needed changing, improving, or modifying ran to about 90 percent.

It becomes clear, then, that lack of agreement between bosses and subordinates about the responsibilities and outputs of the latter can be a serious problem, and that we should consider ways of dealing with it.

SPECIFYING OVERALL GOALS AND OBJECTIVES

Any key executive officer, in attempting to establish the overall performance goals and objectives for his or her organization, must work effectively in three different areas of the organizational structure: the productive use of committees, the effective use of staff, and the functional use of line personnel. Ineffectual utilization of these elements means that overall corporate policies, goals, plans and objectives will not be accurately delegated to subordinates. Let us look at the reasons for some of the problems so many otherwise effective executives have in specifying overall organizational goals and objectives to be accomplished by subordinates.

---

* George S. Ordiorne, *Management and the Activity Trap*, New York: Harper & Row, 1974, p. 28.

Use of Committees

Many people delight in ridiculing committees. Most everyone has heard such statements as: "A camel is a horse that was put together by a committee," or "Committees are made up of the unfit, appointed by the incompetent, to do the unnecessary." However, committees seem to be here to stay in most large organizational structures. And that's just as well, because at higher echelons of management, committees can be used very effectively if the senior-level executives know and understand how. In addition, committees have decided advantages for chief operating executives both in developing corporate policy and helping implement it.

Any effective executive must know how to use a committee, and use it well, if he or she is to be especially competent at delegating work. In order to understand how to use committees, however, it is important to understand their advantages and disadvantages. According to management expert Franklin G. Moore,* the basic advantages in using a committee are that they make possible:

- ☐ Better executive decisions
- ☐ Clarification of thinking
- ☐ Education of those serving on the committee
- ☐ Exchange of information
- ☐ Saving of time
- ☐ Promoting coordination
- ☐ Splintered authority
- ☐ Support by subordinates
- ☐ Support for executives
- ☐ Support of weak executives
- ☐ Blurred responsibility
- ☐ Managerial check reins

Obviously any or all of the above strengths and/or advantages may be derived from using a committee. However, as do most all

---

* Franklin G. Moore, *Management: Organization and Practice*, New York: Harper & Row, 1964, Chapter 20.

things, committees have negative aspects too. Moore lists the more common disadvantages of committees as:

- ☐ Too much talk or irrevelant discussion
- ☐ Inaction and a penchant for postponement
- ☐ Dominance by a few
- ☐ Low-grade or watered down recommendations
- ☐ Political decisions
- ☐ Splitting and diluting of responsibility
- ☐ Development of weaker executives
- ☐ Costliness in terms of executive time and money
- ☐ Stifling of ideas

Obviously, whether a committee is used constructively or destructively depends on the executive who is trying to accomplish a specific task. Since committees are used by top executives to advise, decide, review, plan, and make policy, it is imperative that they know how to use them effectively. If a committee is used poorly, then the executive responsible for it is not doing an effective job of delegating work to it.

Bosses who use committees effectively accomplish a number of things besides the stated purposes of those committees. Some of the secondary effects are more important than others, but all are useful. For example, a committee permits and encourages participation among a number of people, giving them a sense of involvement; it increases opportunities for those who feel that they should have something to say about an operation to say it, instead of feeling frustrated and angry at being bypassed.

When the information or knowledge needed is too great for one person to develop, the best approach to it may be a committee, for a committee can include highly specialized individuals from a number of disciplines who can turn their attention to the common goal. Incidentally, appointment to a committee can be very broadening to such specialists (as well as to egocentric people), since it exposes them to the existence—and importance—of areas other than their own.

Committees are often useful in establishing uniformity of

direction in an organization, since they can resolve matters between separate units and establish performance objectives, selecting among alternatives. Even strong opponents who find themselves on the same committee can serve the purpose of keeping it on the straight and narrow.

Human nature being what it is, committees are especially useful in advising an executive on matters of critical or strategic importance. Their decisions carry far more weight than would those of a single individual—particularly one who is considered autocratic. This works on negative recommendations as well, which helps eliminate proposals that are overly expensive, potentially dangerous to the operation, or otherwise impractical. Even the person whose proposal was rejected by the committee will usually accept that decision, where he or she might oppose rejection by an individual.

Of course, committees should never be asked to consider trivial matters (unless it is to quash a particularly foolhardy idea). In the first place, it wastes the time of too many people; in the second, committees tend to get off the track too easily as it is, and they shouldn't do so over minor issues. Committees should not be expected to administer things, either. They are slow and plodding by nature, not equipped to make quick decisions or take swift action.

When to Use an Individual Rather than a Committee At some time or other, any manager of managers must decide whether to appoint a committee or an individual to handle a given project. As we have said, there are certain advantages to having a committee handle some matters. There are times, however, when it is better —perhaps even essential—to appoint an individual. We assume, of course, that the individual chosen will have the necessary information, judgment, authority, and integrity.

For quick decisions one should always rely on an individual rather than a committee; as mentioned above, a committee is not constituted to move quickly. (Admiral Hyman Rickover is credited with making a statement to the effect that a committee is like "a train on which every passenger has a brake.") In making a decision an individual does not first have to hear (and answer) the arguments of others who may be ego-involved, uninformed, misinformed, or have an ax to grind. True, the individual may miss some useful input that a committee would provide, but our criterion for the individual is that he or she be well informed to start with.

For quick action, by the same reasoning, again it is the individual rather than the committee. It's much simpler for one person to take a particular action than to get several people to do it.

And for accountability, assigning the project to an individual is the only way. So far as a committee is concerned, no one member can be held responsible (either to blame or to praise) above the others. Of course, an individual's decision usually does not carry the same clout as a committee's, but if it is properly supported by the person who appointed the individual in the first place, then it should carry clout enough.

Use of a Staff

Most corporation executives use personal staffs to ensure that their administrative responsibilities are properly met. However, the new manager of managers practically always utilizes his or her personal staff poorly at first (and even some experienced managers of managers don't seem to get the hang of it).

This tendency to use personal staff poorly stems from the fact that until his or her latest promotion, the manager of managers has had very little to do with such personnel. Unless he or she has actually served on a personal staff, his or her only contact with one may have been when, as a supervisor of supervisors, he or she was being ordered by somebody else's staff—personnel, safety, public relations, etc.—to do (or stop doing) this or that.

Now, all of a sudden, the new manager of managers is entitled to a personal staff of his or her own—a staff whose purpose is to help ensure that functional activities are properly carried out by subordinate levels in the organization—and no experience at using one. What to do? How to organize and use them? What is required for—and of—a good personal staff?

Well, to begin with, the staff must be loyal to the executive, and this is one of the several qualities the manager of managers will have to look for in selecting his or her personal staff. The executive must be able to be sure that his or her policies are being carried out in just the way he or she wishes—and to be sure of it without having to follow up everything and breathe down people's necks. But loyalty is a two-way street, and staff members must know that the executive will support them as they perform their numerous functions for him or her. This relationship between the manager of managers and his or her personal staff should not be vague and amorphous; there should be a very real, almost measurable, feeling of mutual trust, respect, and loyalty.

The executive must keep the staff informed of his or her thoughts about the job. The staff simply cannot function effectively unless they know what their boss' policies are and what he or she plans to do about this, that, and/or the other thing. Likewise, the staff must keep the executive informed on what they are thinking about the job, how the projects or assignments for which they are responsible are going, and what plans or expectations they have for these and other job-related matters. Good communications require that both the executive and the staff members be able to make and use reports that are both informative and brief. Many managers of managers facilitate communication by having regularly scheduled meetings with their staff two or three times a week.

One thing that will make both mutual trust and an exchange of information easier is for all staff members to know clearly and exactly their own areas of responsibility *and* those of other staff members. Besides allocating responsibility, this reduces to a minimum the possibility of wasted time, duplication of effort, and trespassing on somebody else's territory. Among those responsibilities—and completely aside from the supervision of projects for the executive—support activities themselves make up an impressive list, including such things as: setting up and maintaining a schedule of internal and external appointments, meetings, conferences, etc.; screening calls and visitors; maintaining tickler files; briefing the executive on visitors; and so on. While the staff should show creativity and initiative, neither its members nor the manager of managers should expect it to assume the latter's responsibility for decision-making.

The staff must be adaptable to the workload and schedule of the manager of managers. Some chief executives are on the road much of the time and some are not, but in either case the staff should be able to provide what the executive needs—plans, information, or results—as he or she needs it. Of course, wherever possible, the good manager of managers will avoid making extreme demands on his or her staff—such as working extraordinary hours or on other than regular working days. And when such demands are unavoidable, he or she will try to compensate the staff member or members of whom they are made—even if that means no more than just saying, "Thank you; I really do appreciate your help."

Proper use of a personal staff can make the manager of managers a far more effective executive than he or she could otherwise be. The staff can assume many of the executive's routine tasks, thereby giving him or her more time to manage committees and line personnel, and to plan, organize, direct, and control.

Use of Line Personnel

Most managers of managers are very effective at dealing with subordinates. Typically, they have come up through the ranks, and they understand intuitively how to get action through other people. Whether or not they can identify them, good managers of managers satisfy the three primary requirements for good face-to-face communication between themselves and supervisors of supervisors:

First, there must be some interface, or point of contact between those things of interest to the manager of managers and those of interest to the supervisor of supervisors. For example, managers of managers talk with production personnel about production, with quality control personnel about quality control, and with both of them about the relationship between quality control and production.

Second, the dialogue between the two parties must be true dialogue; that is, each party must actively listen to the other, even when he or she does not agree with what the other is saying. And for clarity of communication a range of dialogue techniques might be used, supporting face-to-face discussion with written data and audiovisual materials if desired.

Third, there should be a result of this face-to-face meeting. That is, there must be some kind of agreement, not just an exchange of words. If bargaining is required, bargaining should occur, but negotiations should be conducted on an adult basis, moving toward rationally identifiable problems, causes, and solutions.

Any good face-to-face meeting between a manager of managers and his or her immediate subordinates should produce mutual commitment and agreement clear enough to be summarized and confirmed in a subsequent memorandum. The quality of the relationship is important and the roles of the parties need to be understood by each. Constructively handled, this face-to-face relationship should lead to mutual satisfaction on the part of both, and the objectives established should be understood and accepted.

Clarifying Performance Objectives Most managers of managers who have established good interpersonal relationships with their subordinate managers will be effective at delegating work to them. However, experience shows that even experienced managers of managers sometimes fail to get definite commitment to the performance goals they are trying to delegate to their subordinates. Therefore, if the manager of managers is to be effective, performance objectives must be clarified with subordinates. Clarification requires three things: a discussion of what performance goals are required, the reaching of mutual understanding about what is expected, and commitment to the accomplishment of those goals.

Discussion of what is required. As we have said, honest, clear-cut discussion with the subordinate is imperative. How does a manager of managers conduct such a discussion? The following list develops some functional guidelines:

- The manager of managers should let the subordinate know that the subject to be discussed is very important.
- It must be understood that the purpose of this discussion is to determine what work should be done.
- Active listening techniques are used.
- The subordinate should discuss thoroughly the major areas he or she feels are important to the subject.
- The subordinate should be queried about what the manager of

managers could do, refrain from doing, or do differently to help the subordinate accomplish the desired objectives.

- For the manager of managers to tell his or her subordinate supervisor how to do the job is usually bad form, though it may not always be. Unless such instruction is necessary, the discussion should concentrate on the results desired, with only superficial attention to how they should be achieved.
- Any problems anticipated should be brought out into the open and discussed.
- The dialogue should conclude with a summary of the points developed and agreed to. This record can be useful for keeping things straight.

Reaching understanding. It is very difficult for people to fully understand each other's points of view. For example, what is shown in Fig. 11? Is it two X's side-by-side? An M under a W? Something else?

Usually we can understand one another well enough to get along without making an extraordinary effort. Whenever two people are discussing a job assignment, though, it is necessary that they understand each other as completely as possible. For example, the subordinate may say, "Yes, I can have it ready to go by the 15th," and the manager of managers may reply, "OK, that'll be fine." But what happens when the subordinate means that the job will be just ready to leave his or her hands on the 15th and the boss expects to have it in time to do two days of testing and evaluation by the 15th? There will be trouble, and most of it because neither party thought they needed to explain what they meant by "ready to go." After all, everybody knows what "ready to go" means, right? Wrong.

The only practical way to avoid such problems is for the manager of managers and the supervisor of supervisors to sit down and *talk* with each other. And the timing of such talks can be of critical importance; it's much better to make things clear before the job is done than after. The expectations and requirements for any job must be clearly understood by all parties involved before the job

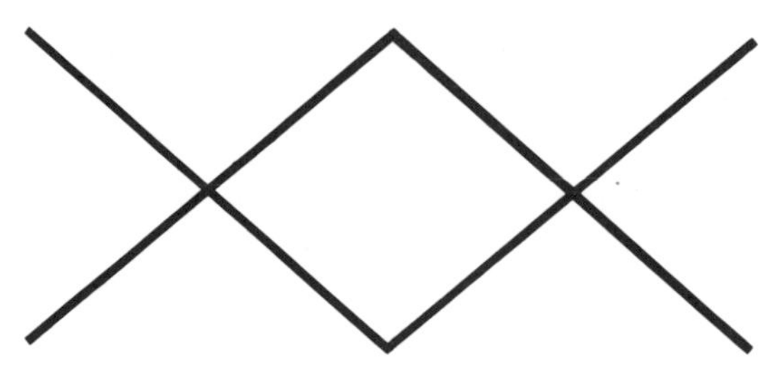

Figure 11

gets under way; the executive must always be ready to convert his or her policy decisions into operational goals.

Obtaining commitment. "Understanding" and "commitment" are two entirely different things. Consider the plight of two sailors whose ship is sinking and who have but one life jacket. They both *understand* that the other wants the jacket, but each is *committed* to getting the jacket for himself.

In an organization, of course, it is necessary that all parties involved be committed to the same goal—say, delivery of one gross of candy-striped blivvets to the loading platform by 8 a.m. Tuesday. Executives need this commitment if they are to accomplish their objectives—and, the truth be known, most subordinates prefer to be committed to something explicit and measurable. It's very encouraging to be able to see the results of one's work.

Being committed means making a promise. In a way, it's like giving a mental IOU to the organization and the individual to whom the performance is being promised. Essentially, the person accepting the assignment says that he or she will cover all the necessary aspects of the job, produce it to the standards required, resolve the various problems and difficulties which arise during its accomplishment, and finish it on schedule.

Being committed means that the individual and the organization become involved with each other. The organization's goals and the individual's personal goals may very well be different, but they must be compatible. If the goals of each are acceptable to the other, then there should be no obstacle to commitment. Greatly oversimplified, the goal of the organization is to manufacture a product (or provide a service); the goal of the worker is to make a living. When the goals of each are acceptable to the other, they work together to achieve them. Actually, while this may be enough for some, many people like to feel that they and their organization are making a contribution to society, and this is in itself a useful motivator.

It should be obvious by now that the managers of managers, in converting policy into operational plans, must be adept at identifying and clarifying goals and objectives to the people who work for him or her, whether they be in committees, on the executive's personal staff, or subordinate supervisors of supervisors. Committee, staff, or line personnel, all should be of great value to the managers of managers in helping him or her be a good and effective administrator.

ASSESSING RESULTS

When managers of managers have difficulty assessing the performance of their subordinates it is usually because they haven't been monitoring the progress of those subordinates or they have not properly controlled the aggressiveness of some of them. At most any level in an organization people will be ambitious and try to get ahead, but this is especially true at the upper levels of management. Aggression is a useful part of ambition, but only if it is controlled and used constructively. The following guidelines can be of value in establishing such control:

- Subordinate managers should be taught to distinguish between what represents true success in the organization and what is only "window dressing." And they should know that the latter can even have a negative effect on their rise in the organization.
- Subordinates should be carefully taught to assess their own performance and to see both themselves and their performance as part of the total organizational environment, to know whether they are helping or hurting themselves and/or the organization.
- Both the manager of managers and the subordinate should be

able to assess where the latter is going, how he or she is going to get there and what he or she might expect to realize on arriving.

- If the subordinate starts to implement a value system of "Me first, organization second, and everybody else last," the manager should not hesitate to set him or her straight, taking punitive steps if necessary.

These guidelines probably will not make it possible to direct every strongly aggressive individual in the organization into constructive channels. However, the astute manager of managers must be willing to apply any and all of them to the task of keeping on the track any individual who is assigned with a particular corporate or organizational responsibility.

Handling the Special Problems of Competitiveness

Competition is a very real motivator, and at the upper levels of any organization it is desired that people be competitive. Competition, in today's business society, allegedly does many desirable things. For example, it:

- Brings about innovation
- Sharpens individual rivalry into superior performance
- Helps force people to work in teams
- Enhances the product quality or service provided to the customer
- Requires that people stretch themselves
- Scuttles inept leadership
- Emphasizes cooperation
- Elicits special skills from special individuals

Competitiveness is generally considered a desirable quality in Western society. Unfortunately, however, people do not always compete on a healthy plane. Competition is fine if the reason for it is that the work is interesting or someone is simply hoping to win something in a nonmalicious sense, but it is unhealthy if it is based on fear of failure, revenge, or other neurotic motives.

The way to cope with good, healthy competition is to recognize the fact that people are competing, and to make sure that they *know* they are competing. In addition, recognition should be given to those who keep their competitive behavior at an acceptable plane. When people produce well on a competitive basis, which includes recognition of the requirements of the team at work, they can grow with the organization.

Unhealthy competition, particularly if it involves groups of managers ganging up on each other, is highly undesirable. It can ruin the morale of an organization; it can even, in the extreme case, ruin the organization. Any manager of managers who has the problem of cliques in his or her organization will do well to handle those cliques as expeditously as possible. Necessarily the effective coping with cliques in an organization requires discovering the nature of the clique, who is involved in it, and its operating techniques, then working through the clique's informal leaders to control or disband it.

Keeping Responsible Subordinate Managers on their Objectives

Any successful manager of managers trying to implement policies knows that his or her objectives must be stated in terms of the results expected from the individual subordinate manager. He or she must also keep the subordinate manager interested in the accomplishment of objectives, and promote interim assessments by the individual of *progress toward* those objectives.

The manager of managers should help subordinates to avoid (or correct) failure, as well as to strive for higher standards of performance as time goes on. Good supervisors know how to do this by setting examples for their subordinates, as well as by insisting that they perform *as they agreed to do* when performance goals were discussed.

Managers of managers know their goals. Sometimes, in measuring performance against those goals, they find that a subordinate has done poorly. This could be because the subordinate was ignorant, it could be because he or she didn't really try, or it could be that the manager of managers failed to define these goals clearly in the first place. Chapter 9 will discuss this subject further.

The Necessity for Critiques

Whenever people fail to accomplish their goals or objectives in an organization, their performance must be critiqued. The critique must be done in good form; its purpose is the improvement of the subordinate's future performance. The critique is not designed to demoralize the subordinate. Any boss can criticize a subordinate but very few can critique properly. However, for a manager of managers the ability to effectively critique a subordinate's performance is essential. The critique can and should be a constructive process which does not demoralize the subordinate or cause resentment. A subordinate supervisor who is badly shaken up could decide to play "Get the boss," and at the executive levels in any organization "Getting the boss" can be a very dangerous game indeed—for everybody involved. Wise managers of managers therefore pay a great deal of attention to the principles expressed in the following list of suggestions, which should be applied in critiquing the performance goals of subordinates:

- ☐ Don't assess *current* performance against *prior* standards.
- ☐ Assess performance standards in terms of what was required by the whole project, not by parts of it.
- ☐ Don't make demands which are inappropriate or which would require impossible levels of performance.
- ☐ Areas where splintered responsibility was possible must not be assessed against an individual's performance goals.
- ☐ Don't emphasize what went wrong, but what can be done to remedy the situation in the future.
- ☐ Don't be reluctant to elaborate upon what performance was expected of the subordinate.
- ☐ Recognize the obstacles which blocked achievement of the goals.
- ☐ Don't ignore any ideas for new goals submitted by the subordinate.
- ☐ Be willing to think through and act upon what the subordinate might suggest would help him or her succeed in the future (assuming, of course, that it is in the purview of his or her performance standards).

- ☐ Don't fail to recognize when the subordinate has seized targets of opportunity or responded effectively when targets were changed by the boss.
- ☐ The boss must not be rigid in knocking out previously agreed upon goals or objectives.
- ☐ Be sure to reinforce successful behavior when the goals are realized.

EXERCISES

1. What are the major pitfalls in using a committee to do anything? How do these problems manifest themselves in your organization?
2. When would you delegate work to a committee? What kinds of constraints would you put on the committee? Why? Are these constraints really a requirement in your organization?
3. What do you feel are the basic strengths of a personal staff? How would you use such a staff in your organization?
4. On what criteria would you pick a personal staff person?

Take the following test on how you deal with a "comer" in your organization who might threaten your job!

When any subordinate encounters "rough waters" in the daily managerial job, generally I:

1. Let him or her ride it out alone—sink or swim.
☐
2. Promptly try to give him or her a hand with the problem, if I can.
☐
3. Break in only when he or she asks for my advice or assistance.
☐

When any report that a subordinate submits to me is less than satisfactory, I:

1. Kick it back with a memo, "You can do better than this."
☐

2. ☐ Try to edit and improve it myself, if I find the time, rather than interrupt the job he or she is on at the time.

3. ☐ Call the subordinate in, identify the weak spots in the report, listen to any rebuttal, and suggest that he or she take another crack at it.

When my subordinate's attitudes toward people seem to irritate them, generally I:

1. ☐ Chalk it up to personality and let nature take its course; the subordinate may change with more experience in dealing with people.

2. ☐ Try to act as peacemaker and assure the people he or she really didn't intend to offend them.

3. ☐ Report the incident to the employee, discuss it, and let him or her do what he or she wants about it.

When one of my people stalls on making a decision on a problem awaiting solution, generally I:

1. ☐ Don't worry about it; the delay is the employee's risk and he or she is accountable.

2. ☐ Urge them to decide on it before things get worse or out of hand.

3. ☐ Think it through with the employee at my request for a confab, but let the employee make his or her own decision at his or her own pace.

When my subordinate takes on a trouble-shooting assignment for me, generally I:

1. ☐ Get the word around to those concerned and leave it to him or her from there on.

2. ☐ Wait until the trouble-shooting job is over, and then pass judgment on how well it was done.

3. ☐ Confer with the employee from time to time to check progress made and problems encountered.

When one of my people appears to be bungling a special project I delegated to him or her, generally I:

1. ☐ Withdraw the delegation before the employee gets in "over his head" any further.

2. ☐ Let the person see it through in the hope he or she will learn from mistakes.

3. ☐ Intercede to see if the employee clearly understands the delegated task and if he or she can get back on the target assignment.

When I observe that one of my employees is not using his or her managerial time wisely, generally I:

1. ☐ Wait until they miss a deadline or neglect an important item, and criticize them.

2. ☐ Break in to remind them of the difference between priorities and routine matters, or what to act on and what to defer.

3. ☐ Point up my observations and try to teach them how to budget their time more effectively as managers. Time is money.

When one of my employees comes up with an idea about which I'm unenthusiastic, generally I:

1. ☐ Brush it off and tell him or her it's best not to rock the boat.

2. ☐ Go through the motions of forwarding it up to my boss or others concerned, with no endorsement on my part.

3. ☐ Discuss it candidly and encourage him or her to think it over and try again; I don't squelch idea germination.

When an employee is working away at a sound organizational change for the department, generally I:

1. ☐ Let him or her hide away to finish until he or she can deliver the whole package.

2. ☐ Check with my superiors to let them know what's "in the works" as to management improvement.

3. ☐ Advise the employee to work on it but to cut in his or her people for their participation and suggestions at the same time.

When a subordinate appears to be running his or her department as a one-man show, generally I:

1. ☐ Allow him or her to "make or break" as he or she sees fit

2. ☐ Alert him or her to the morale problems this can create among his or her people.

3. ☐ Discuss with him or her ways to get more productivity out of people through better utilization of their talents, and have more time for himself or herself for priority management items.

RATING

1. If most of the items you checked were numbered 1, you're not doing well in coaching or bringing along the "comer."
2. If most of the items you checked were numbered 2, you're doing fairly well but tend to blow hot and cold in your coaching responsibility.
3. If most of the items you checked were numbered 3, you are doing a very good job of bring along your "comer."

Assess your key subordinates by using the following checklist:

Rating as to effectiveness in the following:	Consistently very good	Generally adequate	Can stand good deal of improvement
Keeps me informed.	☐	☐	☐
Saves my time and energy.	☐	☐	☐
Capitalizes on opportunities.	☐	☐	☐
Handles good share of the tough problems himself or herself.	☐	☐	☐
Acts as the "chief" in my absence.	☐	☐	☐
Relieves me of the paperload.	☐	☐	☐
Runs interference for me.	☐	☐	☐
Makes decisions for himself or herself.	☐	☐	☐
Takes on and completes delegated assignments.	☐	☐	☐
Improves the general image of his or her department or my office.	☐	☐	☐
Handles new ideas and proposals.	☐	☐	☐

Enables me to meet deadlines and crash-job requirements.	☐	☐	☐
Communicates down the line goals, orders, instructions, and evaluations of progress.	☐	☐	☐
Smokes out trouble situations and arranges for trouble-shooting to be done.	☐	☐	☐
Represents the department in liaison with others within and outside the organization.	☐	☐	☐
Helps me build a good management team among subordinate managers.	☐	☐	☐
Allocates the use of his or her own time.	☐	☐	☐
Handles his or her own job—plus.	☐	☐	☐

WHY TOP EXECUTIVES SOMETIMES FAIL AT DELEGATION

According to authors Ernest Dale and L. C. Michelon,* (1) once people become managers, they must also become organizers; (2) unless managers organize the work of their subordinates, those subordinates will be getting in each other's way (even countering each other's efforts); and (3) the way the manager organizes work has a great deal to do with the effort his or her employees put into their jobs.

Good organizers who are effective at delegating work to their subordinates know just what is to be accomplished, by whom, and under what circumstances. Unfortunately, as was pointed out in the preceding chapter, at top levels in many organizations, delegation of jobs to individuals is not always done well. One of the reasons for this is that many higher levels of executives, especially managers of managers, don't fully understand what delegation at their level is all about. They intuitively feel that they should be able to do better, yet in many cases don't know how. All too often their problem centers on the difficulty they (like others) may have in distinguishing between "doing" tasks and performance objectives.

Dale and Michelon suggest that any manager of managers who is concerned about his or her ability to differentiate between tasks and objectives might try the following simple test: Pick out, at random, any employee who reports directly to the manager of managers and ask him or her (tactfully and in a nonoffensive manner) what it is that he or she (the subordinate) does to justify being on the payroll. Dale and Michelon argue (and certainly this author's experience will concur) that the supervisor of supervisors will probably reply by stating what he or she *does* rather than what he or she is *accomplishing* on the job; such things as "We process grievances filed by the union," or "We ensure that the product that goes out the door comes within all our quality assurance specifications and governmental regulations," or the like. Such statements indicate that the individuals making them are still thinking in terms of task orientation—what they actually *do* rather than what they accomplish or contribute. Yet contribution to the organization,

* Ernest Dale and L. C. Michelon, *Modern Management Methods*, Cleveland: World Publishing Company, 1966, p. 31.

in terms of the results expected, is what an objectives-oriented manager would suggest.

It can be argued that the biggest reason why top-level executives fail at delegating is that they are not total-project-oriented (and therefore fail to assign overall project accomplishment to their subordinates) or that the subordinate is thinking in terms of too small-scale, task-oriented functions rather than total operational objectives. Let's take a look at some of the shortcomings of managers of managers in this respect, then consider some of the problems which occur to the supervisor of supervisors.

SHORTCOMINGS OF THE EXECUTIVE

In criticizing the upper levels of management in many of our larger organizations one must necessarily be slightly cautious about what one says. After all, most people who arrive at these levels are hard-working, honest, and intelligent, and otherwise possess many of the admirable traits of most people in our society. Yet many fail to effectively utilize the people who are working for them.

In examining the careers of experienced managers of managers we find that it *is* possible for good executives to get optimum performance from subordinates. Certainly there are failures; human beings do make mistakes. And occasionally there have been executives in both industry and public life with psychological and/or physiological problems that hampered their executive ability. But usually the executive's difficulties with delegation arise from the nature of the job, and from the problems attendant on determining goals and the means of achieving them. These problems occur more frequently to new managers of managers than to more experienced ones. However, old dogs, too, may need to learn new tricks.

Lack of Clear Goals

William M. Batten, as chairman of the J. C. Penney Company, is reported to have offered the following advice: "Get the facts. Explore alternatives. Make the detailed study. Plan. After that, the decisions just leap out at you."

Being able to determine where one wants to go and how to get there—to conduct operational planning, if you will—is the benchmark for success at the manager-of-managers level in any organization. According to management experts Joel Ross and Michael J. Kami,* there are ten commandments for effective management, all of them essentially arguing for clearcut development of operational strategies and objectives if one is to be successful at the corporate-policy level. These commandments include:

- □ Developing and communicating a unified strategy under which all members of the organization can function.
- □ Establishing controls and overall operational constraints.
- □ Requiring that functional directors be actively involved in overall management of the organization.
- □ Avoiding one-man rule of the operation.
- □ Establishing management depth.
- □ Being adaptive to change.
- □ Being alert to customer's needs *and power.*
- □ Not misusing information inputs.
- □ Not engaging in accounting manipulations.
- □ Developing an organizational structure responsible to the needs of the personnel who work for the organization.

Ross and Kami's maxims tend to hold true, at least in their assessment of why *top*-level executives in large corporations throughout the world have failed. They clearly document the claim that many chief executives have failed in recent years because of their own ineptness at defining clearly just what they intended to accomplish—that is, their goals. Most of those who read this book can recall cases they have heard of in which the failure of executives to define goals has had costly—even almost disastrous—effects on this organization or that.

In any organization, failure to define goals at the operational level limits the executive's ability to delegate. Without clearly defined goals, how far down the line is it feasible to push responsibility upon subordinates? And at what point does the supervisor of supervisors have enough information to make decisions that will

---

* Joel E. Ross and Michael J. Kami, *Corporate Management in Crisis: Why the Mighty Fall*, Englewood Cliffs, N.J.: Prentice-Hall, 1973, p. 21.

affect total organizational goals? (For example, a production manager could not tell what effect a change in product design would have on either sales or profits unless he or she and the sales manager could assess the situation with the comptroller. And the request for such consultative integration must be backed by the manager of managers.)

One reason why Management by Objectives appeals to top-level managers is that it forces them to define operational goals and objectives for the organization rather than to concentrate on tasks. Author Edward C. Schleh* has suggested several guidelines which are used by managers of managers in defining performance goals and objectives for their subordinates. They include: making goals realistic, writing down and cross-checking to see that all goals blend together, requiring that objectives appear fair to the individuals to whom they are assigned (and who are to become responsible for them), insisting that subordinates accomplish all objectives assigned to them, and keeping the objectives assigned fairly simple. Discussion with senior-level operating executives by this author would indicate virtually unanimous agreement with these requirements.

Failure to Utilize Resources

This should not be confused with *lack* of resources, which is a different matter all together—and sometimes easier to fix, since the chief executives in most organizations can usually get what they need one way or another. What we are talking about are cases in which the human, material, and financial resources needed for a job are available—but not properly utilized.

One of the major causes of this problem is simply the failure to properly define goals. If the goals are not clearly understood, the means of achieving them cannot be readily identified. It is not enough to say, "Go cut down a tree." But if we say, "Go cut down a small sapling," then the subordinate has enough information to choose among the available resources—and will take a hatchet, leaving the three-foot chain saw for someone who really needs it.

Another cause of failure to utilize resources is simply lack of

---

* Edward C. Schleh, *Management by Results*, New York: McGraw Hill, 1961.

imagination. As a supervisor of supervisors, the person who is now a manager of managers did many things in certain ways that he or she had found to work satisfactorily. But those ways may not necessarily work for the manager of managers, and to stick with the tried and true may be to waste resources or otherwise use them improperly. Certainly some of the old methods may still be good; we are not recommending that they be discarded arbitrarily, but the manager of managers should examine them (and all new ideas as well) with an active imagination. The same applies to similar problems in different organizations; the best way to ventilate the paint shop at Amalgamated Anchorbolts, Inc., may be the worst way at World-Wide Widgets.

Lack of imagination affects not only choice between obvious alternative resources but also recognition of resources that are not so obvious. People are resources, for example, and good managers of managers are willing to develop younger people in the organization, not being at all afraid of young "comers." Furthermore, they are willing to pay attention to what their suppliers and customers can do for them, both in a physical sense and in an advisory capacity. Practically always they will make a concerted effort to release the human potential available to them. Further, they don't overly centralize and/or proceduralize their activities because they know full well that to do so stifles initiative and innovation from subordinates. In addition, they try to keep abreast of changes in methods, products, technology, and salesmanship. Also, they are totally aware of how the individuals who work for them fit into the system. And finally, they tailor that system to the needs of their operational unit. When they have this vision, of course, they are in a position to effectively delegate or assign work to key people within the organization.

Lack of Personal Commitment

It probably is not fair to say that many managers of managers are not personally committed to the success of the organization for which they work. Practically always the problem at upper levels of management is that people may be *too* dedicated or *too* committed to the success of the organization—and to some individuals, including themselves, within it.

What we are talking about is lack of personal commitment to the operational goals and objectives the organization must achieve. This particular problem is not exactly rampant among managers of managers, but, particularly in large organizations, there are always people who disagree about what the "big boss" actually ought to accomplish. The result is foot-dragging and lack of commitment to overall organizational policies.

Good top-level management talent is important in running a business. It is no coincidence that, year after year, *Dun's Review and Modern Industry* identifies management depth as one of the primary characteristics of the ten best-managed companies in the United States. Invariably certain companies reappear on the list of those best managed, and many others seldom, if ever, even get honorable mention. Obviously, there are a number of factors involved in the appearance of any company on such a list, but one of those factors—and an important one—is the degree to which its executive personnel are committed to the policies of the organization.

Failure to get commitment at the manager-of-managers level can be serious. Probably more often than not it occurs because of genuine differences of opinion about where the organization ought to be going and how it should get there. But whether the purpose of the organization is altruistic (as with feeding the starving) or selfish (as with simply making the owners rich) it cannot be fully effective—and may even fail entirely—without the commitment of its executive personnel to its goals.

Intolerance of Ambiguity

Managerial consultants and executive confidants are often in a position to observe that the people who get to the top—who become managers of managers—have their goals and drives very firmly fixed in their minds. This tends to lead to a similar firmness in their opinions about how things should be done. Further, a manager of managers almost invariably has total confidence in his or her own skills, talents, methods, and abilities—and often little or no confidence in those of his or her subordinates.

Knowing how one wants things is OK, short of being inflexible about it, and a manager of managers should be self-confident.

But a good executive should be confident enough to live with ambiguity, to be able to say, "No, I don't know *exactly* how that job stands right this minute—but I've got someone who does, someone I know to be qualified and capable." The manager of managers who does not allow himself or herself to feel that way will probably handle delegation in one of three ways:

1. Doesn't delegate. This wastes the time, talent, and ability the subordinate is contributing and the salary he or she is being paid. It wastes the time the manager of managers spend on doing what should be a subordinate's work and the salary the organization pays him or her for *managing*.
2. Underdelegates. Nearly as bad, because the subordinate works on only *part* of a problem instead of the whole problem. There is still a great waste of the subordinate's abilities and salary and an increase in the probability of error and duplication of effort.
3. Overdelegates. Also no good, since in overdelegating the manager of managers hems in the subordinate with overexplicit definition of the job and how to do it, and also insists on participating in (or even usurping) decisions that should be the subordinate's province. Again, wasteful of the time and talent of both parties.

All three of these approaches to delegation are very bad for morale. They imply that the subordinate is not skilled or experienced or trustworthy enough to be allowed to handle the job alone, and that, in fact, he or she may not be quite competent to fill his or her present position, let alone advance beyond it.

Since this type of executive must know what is going on at all times, he or she will insist on many and detailed reports and controls. Writing up the former takes too much time from the supervisor of supervisors and defining and applying the latter takes too much time from the manager of managers.

As deadlines draw near, the "low-ambiguity-tolerance" boss gets increasingly "antsy," demanding more and more information from his or her subordinate and, if problems arise, showing a tendency to blow his or her stack. All this cannot help but have a negative effect on morale and costs—and probably on production as well. To turn matters around, the manager of managers will have to learn to live with the fact that, in organizational as well as private life, a certain amount of ambiguity is unvoidable—and that it is tolerable enough when one has confidence in one's subordinates.

Customers Who Want to "Go to the Top"

This problem, which interferes with the proper delegation of work and responsibility, may sometimes be beyond the control of the manager of managers and even that of the organization itself. It is unfortunate, but it is a fact, that some customers and other people from outside the organization are unwilling to deal with anyone but top management. When deliveries cannot be met or price concessions made, when "official" information is required by union leaders or the press, or when financial commitments must be made, these people insist on hearing it all from "the horse's mouth."

Of course, if the customer requiring this top-level contact is a very important individual or the representative of some organization that carries considerable weight with the executive's own organization, then the executive may very well get involved and do whatever "hand-holding" is necessary to keep the customer happy. Ordinarily, however, the manager of managers will try to train the customer to deal directly with the subordinate who is responsible for that information or part of the organization in which the customer is interested. Senior executives, after all, are not usually familiar with the details of any given department's operation—*and there is no reason why they should be.* That is the responsibility of their subordinates, who are supposedly capable and well-informed in their own areas. So when a customer insists on dealing directly with the manager of managers, the chances are that that executive will, in turn, refer to one of his or her subordinates, which of course the customer could—and should—have done in the first place.

As we have seen, when managers of managers are ineffectual at delegating work to subordinates, it is sometimes because of functional situations they truly cannot avoid, and sometimes for psychological reasons. Their most common problems are associated with sophisticated, albeit commonplace, managerial practices—planning, organizing, directing, and controlling—and must be coped with in ways different from those by which a direct supervisor or a supervisor of supervisors would approach similar problems. The penalties for failure to handle those problem areas effectively are quite severe in some cases, so it is essential that the manager of managers clearly recognize and understand these delegation pitfalls.

SHORTCOMINGS OF THE SUBORDINATE

Managers of managers are not solely responsible for the many problems they have in delegating effectively, nor do outside influences account for them all. Some of the problems are contributed (probably mostly by accident, but sometimes intentionally) by supervisors of supervisors. These subordinates have their own attitudes and ambitions, after all, and work under their own physiological and psychological conditions. As in other human relationships, these factors are bound to have various effects on those for whom the supervisors of supervisors work, and for the rest of this chapter we will consider some of the causes of these effects.

Deliberate Withholding of Cooperation

In any organization, people seldom deliberately refuse to cooperate with the manager of managers unless such refusal is based on a serious difference of opinion about operational policy or ethical considerations. Most commonly it is the former; both industry and government can supply many instances in which a subordinate's opinion about operational policy so differed from that of the manager of managers that the subordinate said, in effect, "I cannot continue to work for you unless this condition is changed to be more acceptable to me." Such a situation does not necessarily reflect discredit on either party; more than likely it is simply an honest and sincere disagreement between two hard-working people who are knowledgeable and experienced in their field and are dedicated to it.

In most circumstances, of course, open and genuine disagreement is no problem at all. Those who assess theoretical issues associated with conflict resolution say that in healthy organizations such genuine, open differences of opinion encourage creativity and lead to the resolution of problems. However, old-style pragmatists often cannot cope with such open conflict and don't appreciate it at all.

But what do managers of managers do when they encounter subordinates who deliberately withdraw cooperation because of genuine differences of opinion? Are they justified in reacting heavy handedly? The value systems of our Western culture teach that in resolving disagreement, the most usual arrangement is that one party must win and the other must lose. Since neither party wants to be the loser, each feels free to use authority or other means of coercion to win. The result, of course, is conflict.

A major trouble with settling a conflict on a win-lose basis (aside from the hard feelings this is likely to create) is that neither party may have the best possible solution. Executives with experience at working with conflict know that the best—the most constructive—way of dealing with it is for them to be as mature, objective, and open as possible and assume the role of problem-solver. In doing so, many managers of managers have found the following guidelines (which of course are not the only ones) to be very helpful:

- Focus all attention and discussion on the goals being sought by the organization rather than simply looking for the handiest solution.
- Be objective about the positions taken by the individual antagonists rather than judgmental about their personal or professional qualities.
- Talk in terms of specific goal accomplishment rather than in generalities (such as flag, motherhood, and other uncontrollable variables like weather). And make sure that those specifics deal with things that can be changed or are negotiable, not with hard and fast rules that cannot be altered.
- Consider the motives of each individual who is giving and receiving information in the conflct; try to understand each side's point of view.
- Depersonalize the issues and avoid making judgments about

the "rightness" or "wrongness" of any issue or problem being discussed.

- ☐ Recognize that disagreement frequently leads to creativity, so long as it doesn't make people feel *threatened* or *defensive* about the position they have taken.
- ☐ Broaden choices into problems. Asking "Which do you want to do, A or B?" restricts the possibilities. Better to ask, "Just what do you want to accomplish?"
- ☐ Avoid trade-offs, such as voting, averaging, flipping coins, dividing up territory, or other arbitrary methods of compromise.
- ☐ Try not to control people's feelings by use of moral suasion or other techniques. Rather try to focus on *understanding* the points of view held by others in the organization (be they the subordinate or the superior).
- ☐ Develop discussion which will aid in the definition of the problem, the search for solutions to it, and the assessment or evaluation of the available alternatives.

Many good managers of managers have found these guidelines to be most effective in helping resolve issues between managers of managers and supervisors of supervisors. This is true even when there is malice involved in the disagreement. They will practically always work when there is a genuine, sincere difference of opinion based on realistic differences and/or misunderstandings.

Lack of Ambition to Advance

In almost any organization there are those who seem uninterested in advancing beyond a certain point, whose "get up and go has got up and went." There are numerous reasons for this attitude: Some people feel that they've been taken—by the boss, or by the organization, or by life in general—and decide that since their performance and abilities are not appreciated, they will just sit it out from that point on. Others feel that there is so little room at the top that the odds against reaching it are overwhelming, and so there's little point in driving for it. And yet others feel that though the top may be accessible to them, and they qualified for it, the effort and dedication required to reach it are more than the position is worth. "Life is too short," they say, "Who wants to be the richest one in the cemetery?"

For one reason or another, then, many people do lose their motivation to advance. Psychologists point out that this change in attitude usually begins to appear in a person's middle working years (say from age 35 to 50), years during which most people arrive at, or become established in, responsible positions as supervisors of supervisors or perhaps lower-level managers of managers. This pattern has become so clear that one major corporation conducted a motivation study of *all* their executives over the age of 52. They found that beyond that age very few, *if any,* of their supervisors of supervisors or managers of managers actually accomplished a great deal, and that they *almost never* undertook anything really new or different or earth-shattering. Essentially it seemed that the attitude of these executives was "Don't rock the boat," and that as they approached the age of 60 their principal motivation was to put in their time and get a good retirement from the organization.

We mentioned earlier (Chapter 3) Zeigarnik's findings that while people often are not highly motivated to *start* a project, they usually are highly motivated to *finish* it. There is, for all of us, satisfaction in completing a job which lets us feel that we have accomplished something. In order to establish motivation, then, the effective manager of managers will attempt to assign tasks that are (or can be made to be) project oriented, with clearly defined performance goals. Also, he or she will make those assignments in a manner consistent with the ideas developed in Chapter 8, which suggest procedures for clarifying performance objectives.

The Nonachievement Syndrome

Whether or not there is such a thing in medical terms, the nonachievement syndrome is real enough in organization management. And it doesn't refer to the people we've just been discussing, who might better be described as "resting on their oars." No, what we're talking about now is the fact that some people simply are *not* motivated.

People who become supervisors of supervisors or managers of

managers are, as we have said, highly motivated. If they become nonachievers, people who *will not* assume the responsibilities that go with their position, then probably something traumatic has happened to them. Depending on the individual it may be something in their private life or it may be an on-the-job problem; it may require professional counseling or it may require that the individual and the organization go their separate ways.

A serious study made by the author a few years ago* found that in dealing with managers who have succumbed to the nonachievement syndrome, most organizations tend to be more lenient than is good either for themselves or for the executives involved. In fact, most larger organizations in this country commonly do not fire, demote, or otherwise seriously disenfranchise supervisors of supervisors or managers of managers who have come to perform unsatisfactorily. Their justifications for failing to take such actions range from the more or less reasonable to the more or less ridiculous:

- ☐ Through training and counseling the organization can redevelop the person involved so that he or she will no longer be an unsatisfactory performer.
- ☐ The organization is so big that the unsatisfactory performer can be transferred from one job to another until a spot can be found where he or she can function satisfactorily.
- ☐ The organization simply has a de facto policy against firing.
- ☐ Not firing anyone is good public relations for the organization.
- ☐ The organization's selection techniques are so well defined that it never hired anyone who could not do an acceptable job. (In other words, the manager's unsatisfactory performance is not really unsatisfactory after all, no matter what the records show.)

---

* See Lawrence L. Steinmetz, *Managing the Marginal and Unsatisfactory Performer*, Reading, Mass.: Addison-Wesley, 1969.

For the manager of managers to be unwilling to deal with the problem of the nonachiever is inexcusable. Sooner or later the situation will become intolerable, bad feelings will develop, and the nonachiever will *have* to be fired. Firing the unsatisfactory performer, however unpleasant it may be, is not the worst thing that can happen to him or her—and certainly not to the organization—but it should be done before hard feelings develop or the individual's or the organization's ability to function is impaired irrevocably. If firing is the best solution, and the step is not taken, everybody loses: The unsatisfactory performer is practically always unhappy, continually complaining that he or she is not appreciated; the organization gets no productivity from that individual (who may even affect productivity negatively); and the executive under whom he or she serves (and who should have dealt with the situation) is in an impossible position. There is no justification for failing to come to grips with the problem of an individual who has become so much the nonachiever that he or she cannot accept assignments delegated to him or her.

The last portion of this chapter has been devoted to the question of what happens when subordinates at the supervisor-of-supervisors level fail to shoulder the responsibilities assigned to them by their bosses. To some degree this is a result of genuine, open differences of opinion. This requires that the manager of managers assume a problem-solving role. At other times, however, subordinates fail to shoulder responsibility because they lack ambition to advance. It was argued that things such as the Zeigarnik effect and achievement motivation are the true motivators of individuals who are only marginally inspired. It was also pointed out that some people are totally unsatisfactory performers, being unwilling and incapable of handling the responsibilities their superiors delegate to them. Such cases practically always require a heavy handed response. A review of the goals of top management levels in many of the more dynamic organizations in the United States will aptly demonstrate that they commonly trim their dead wood, while those organizations which are much less dynamic do not—they leave it right on the tree, where it can hinder growth.

EXERCISES

Work through the following questions to determine whether you and your organization need to delegate more.

	Yes	No
1. Do older people predominate in key positions, especially at the middle levels?	☐	☐

How did this come about?

New policies to consider:

2. Is there a shortage of people trained to take over key places in case of deaths or resignation?	☐	☐

Positions where this is the case:

Actions to start regarding this:

3. Are key personnel so tied to their jobs that they lack time to take part in commmunity services and other public-relations activities?	☐	☐

	Yes	No
Who are these people?		

This could be changed by:

4. Are some individuals filling two or more key spots?	☐	☐

Who and why?

Possible job realignments are:

5. Are key personnel so occupied by current details that they cannot plan future moves, thus causing the firm to move slowly in meeting competition or in changing markets or processes?	☐	☐

Examples:

	Yes	No
Remedies to consider:		
6. Are key personnel spending part of their time in actual production work? Who? Their positions could be reorganized by:	☐	☐
7. Are key personnel under such tight control they are afraid to delegate? Examples: Other controls which might be used are:	☐	☐
8. Are key personnel who have been promoted still carrying details from their previous jobs?	☐	☐

	Yes	No
Who?		
What details?		
Plan for restructuring their positions:		
9. Do standard practices, job simplification, rules, and procedures work against delegating in the enterprise?	☐	☐
Which practices, etc.?		
Alternative arrangements might be:		
10. Is the ratio of private secretaries and "assistants to" below average?	☐	☐
The gains and losses from this are:		

	Yes	No
Areas where this might be changed:		
11. Is decision-making (plans, methods, job problems, etc.) restricted to a few individuals or specialists?	☐	☐
Examples:		
Decision-making could safely be broadened by:		
12. Is official criticism of errors so strong that key people hesitate to show initiative or take risks?	☐	☐
Examples:		
Possible changes worth trying:		
13. Are key personnel pitted against each other, so that they strive to win personal credit rather than to build a team?	☐	☐

	Yes	No

Examples:

Policy changes this suggests:

14. Is it the practice to promote hard workers or "balls of fire" before they have developed understudies to take their places? ☐ ☐

Examples:

This might be done differently by:

15. Has it been necessary to go outside the firm to find replacements for key personnel? ☐ ☐

Examples:

What policy reconsiderations does this suggest?

	Yes	No
16. Do capable younger employees resign before their full abilities can be used by the firm?	☐	☐

Examples:

This suggests that we should:

17. Do the rank and file of workers seem to lack initiative?	☐	☐

Possible policy reason for this:

Actions that might change it:

18. Do production workers seem to lack job interest, or lack satisfaction with what they do on their jobs?	☐	☐

Examples:

	Yes	No
Delegating might help this by:		
19. Does the firm have the reputation of being a one-man company, or has life insurance, payable to the firm, been taken out on some key personnel but not others?	☐	☐

Who?

Long-range problems this poses are:

10

DELEGATION IN THE STAFF, TECHNICAL, AND PROFESSIONAL ENVIRONMENT

No book on the art and skill of delegation would be complete without devoting some attention to the special problems of delegating effectively to staff, technical, or professional personnel.

Many people who are involved in these areas feel that their work is different from other, more "ordinary" kinds of work. In his research, Lee. E. Danielson* found that *whether or not* engineers and scientists are different *as a group*, they certainly *perceive* themselves to be different (and intend or want to be managed differently). Similar studies show that others, in various professional or select groups, also think of themselves as different and worthy of being bossed or managed in a particular way.

The job of delegating work to people in staff, technical, or professional positions *is* to some degree different from delegation in less specialized areas. A microbiologist or a personnel specialist (or anyone else who is technically highly skilled) must be performing (or be in charge of) technical functions. This means that he or she is engaged in a type of "doing" work, just as is the line worker, for example. However, the nature of this work is greatly different from that of the work done by the line worker. For the most part it involves more thinking, creativity, and intellectual curiosity, not to mention the more rigorous aspects of scientific methodology, the law, or other esoteric matters.

Intellectual activity, though it very often has material results, is not measured in specific units of output—such as distance, volume, or weight. It is, therefore, difficult to supervise the work of and individual engaged in intellectual activity. And the more intellectual the work, the more difficult the supervision. When we earlier discussed span of control we said that anyone can effectively supervise work which is relatively simple and can also be closely and directly observed. Intellectual work—usually performed by professional and technical individuals and requiring the powers of deductive and inductive reasoning—limits the supervisor's span of control.

People who manage scientsts and engineers know that the problem of assigning work and getting results from these individu-

---

* Lee E. Danielson, *Characteristics of Engineers and Scientists*, Ann Arbor, Mich.: Bureau of Industrial Relations, 1960.

als is very involved, and sometimes exceedingly difficult. Nevertheless, some statement can be made about how the manager in the highly technical or professional work environment can delegate work to responsible individuals and obtain the required results.

DELEGATING WORK IN STAFF, TECHNICAL, AND PROFESSIONAL AREAS

As mentioned above, the delegation of work in the staff, technical, and professional areas presents its own problems. Some of these problems derive from the nature of the work, others from the attitudes of the individuals doing the work and yet others by the system in which the work is performed. Let us consider some examples of these problems.

Professionalism and Immunity to Certain Job Assignments

Many writers have tried to pinpoint the special differences between employees who are creative and/or professional and those who are not. The more commonly mentioned differences can be summarized as follows:

- *High motivation.* Practically always it is claimed that creative, professional personnel are more highly motivated, at least so far as their own discipline is concerned. Because of this they are said to be different, and to consider themselves as both different *and* more valuable employees.
- *Openness to feelings.* Those involved in highly technical and professional fields (including staff work) tend to feel they are more open to opinions and ideas that differ from their own. Usually this openness is attributable to their intellectual curiosity or their respect for scientific methodology. Because of it they feel that they are better able to express and/or understand the feelings of other individuals in the organization.
- *Active curiosity.* This is considered a hallmark of difference between highly technical and creative people and the rest of the world. Because of their intellectual curiosity they presumably are more interested in the things going on about them. This quality is most commonly attributed to technical people, it being argued that they develop their skills as the result of

having to be keen observers of both physical and intellectual phenomena.

- *Psychological isolation.* Many staff, technical, and professional people consider themselves psychologically isolated from others. This is not necessarily by design, but may be the result of their work interests, which in various instances tends to force some degree of isolation upon them.
- *Persistence.* Tenacity of purpose, at least in resolving problems or acquiring information about one's work interests, is also claimed to be one of the more unique dimensions of staff, technical, and professional people. It is suggested that such people often won't let go of projects as soon as they should.
- *High tolerance for ambiguity.* Most highly trained staff, technical, and professional people feel that they have a higher degree of tolerance for ambiguity and uncertainty than do other workers. Because of this they often feel that they can cope with variables which are not clearly defined or not easily resolved by others.
- *Sensitivity.* Many people who have worked with professional or technically trained individuals will testify that such people are more sensitive than most and, as a result, often are easily offended. Some even argue that such people tend to be highly emotional, demonstrating volatile personalities, and given to outbursts of temper.
- *Originality.* People trained in professional and technical disciplines not only consider themselves original and creative, but also take a great pride in their intuition, feelings, and critical judgment. This talent for originality supposedly enables them to handle ideas with great facility.
- *Fluency.* Highly intellectual people are, almost necessarily, highly fluent people. There is little argument that staff, technical, and professional people are usually able to articulate their feelings easily.
- *Flexibility.* Some people feel that the work done by engineers, scientists, and other technically trained staff people requires

them to be highly flexible and adaptive. However, others who have worked with technical people argue that they are quite inflexible and adapt poorly, if at all, to organizational requirements.

Because professional and highly trained technical and staff people are presumably different from others, many people argue that they should be immune from certain organizational constraints and requirements. In the author's experience, however, experienced managers and supervisors of highly trained staff, technical, and professional people would not argue that they should be immune to the normal rules which apply at any level of management. Job assignments and delegation of work should be handled just as with anyone else, but an assessment of the uniqueness of the work requirements and consequent job dictates is usually deemed reasonable.

One study has found that of people who work in a supervisory capacity over scientists and engineers, five out of eight feel that their groups are *not* different from others. But of those who feel that their groups are unique, most have tried to establish exceptional polices for managing them. Usually they develop professional hierarchies in their organizations, as distinct from managerial or production hierarchies, because otherwise the organization's production and sales people would be paid more than its technical and professional personnel. In practice, then, there is much disagreement about whether technical and professional people should be treated differently from others in an organization.

Indifference Toward Organizational Goals

Most executives working for giant corporations are prone to be results-oriented. Essentially their attitude is that people who are getting the results that are required can be treated virtually any way they want to be treated. But if they are not, the executives feel that "something should be done."

The truth be known, the feelings of staff, technical, and professional people toward organizational goals probably are not much different from those of other people. Yet, to some degree, their motivations and ambitions are different. Charles Hughes and M. Scott Myers of Texas Instruments, in some of their well-known research, have found that the motivational interests of scientists and engineers are to some degree different from those of hourly male technicians and female assemblers. But they also found that there is a similarity of motivational interest among *scientists, engineers,* and *manufacturing supervisors.*

Essentially, it should be recognized that motivational drives and ambitions of staff, technical, or professional people are mostly derived from the work they are doing. It is true that the jobs and functions of scientific and engineering people and of highly trained staff and professional people are different from those of manufacturing or production people. As a result, their motivational interests are different—and those differences must be recognized if a manager is to delegate work to them effectively. Some of these motivational differences are assessed in the following paragraphs:

Career values. Inevitably the career value systems of highly technical and creative people—as well as staff personnel—are different from the values of others. Charles Hughes and Richard Flowers have found that technically trained people are a good deal more existential in their outlook toward what they are trying to do and accomplish at work than are typical, "career-oriented" executives. Because of this their aspirations toward their careers and life-long ambitions toward money, titles, position, etc., are decidedly different. This must be understood by the manager who is trying to accomplish work through a subordinate.

Challenging and stimulating work. Scientific, engineering, staff, or other technical people expect more challenging and stimulating work than do other people. The original work of Frederick Herzberg, for example, underscored the fact that people with engineering backgrounds desire work which is challenging to them and gives them a feeling of accomplishment and achievement.

Greater responsibility and advancement. Highly technically trained people like responsibility and usually say they want more of it, particularly in those areas in which they are expert. Also, for the most part, they want to advance in their careers. However, it should be understood that by "advancement" they refer not so much to the power and money which managerial and executive personnel have as to recognition for technical competence and expertise.

Training and education. Scientists and engineers do tend to place a high premium on intellectual achievement. Because of this, training sessions and educational facilities designed to foster, promote, and develop ideas and knowledge about the world and what goes on in it are seen as being extremely important. The manager must understand the motivations of highly technical people for academic and intellectual achievements, as well as their curiosity, accomplishments, and interests. Good delegation skills thus enable the delegate to go after the realization of these expectancies of the job.

Working conditions and facilities. It goes without saying that people value good working conditions and facilities. However, ample research in the 1960's and early 1970's has pointed out that while poor working conditions can be demotivational, good working conditions *in and of themselves* are not motivational. Technical and professional people have different ideas about what they expect from work and working conditions, but, as we have said, whether they deserve any special kind of treatment is still debated. It is certainly true that they will react differently to many conventional kinds of organizational constraints. Consequently, they may either accept their assigned work in a very open and straightforward fashion or they may resist it strongly.

Types of Work Resistance

Staff, technical, and professional people do not often avoid work assigned to them, and when they do it is rarely because they don't understand what is being delegated. In fact, so far as understanding of the work is concerned, one of the problems with many highly technical and professional people is that they read *more* into an assignment than they should. When they *do* resist an assignment, then, it is likely to be for some idiosyncratic reason that has nothing to do with their ability to understand and perform the assigned task. Let us examine some of the positions that highly technical and professional people sometimes assume that lead them to resist work assignments.

The prima donna. In any professional environment there are, practically always, some people who become prima donnas. The reason for this, in the minds of many managerial consultants who have observed it, is that these people have an extremely high regard for job knowledge and understanding, tending often to overemphasize the value of the creative process and their intellectual capabilities. Practically always such people feel that their high competence in their specialty somehow places them above the common work-a-day problems with which others must cope.

What does it take to work effectively with a prima donna? Essentially, tact in assigning responsibilities and jobs to him or her. And tact should be based on a compassionate understanding of the strengths, weaknesses, fears, motivations, and idiosyncracies of the person being supervised. Those who are successful at supervising the prima donna practically always have a very tolerant and respectful awareness of that individual's achievements, frustrations, and aggravations. They neither overrate nor undervalue, belittle nor exaggerate the prima donna's contribution. Basically they divert the attention of the prima donna from that special class in which he or she claims membership to an attitude of "Where are we going now?" Emphasis is placed on goal accomplishments rather than the doing of (menial) tasks.

Some supervisors find that a sensitive response to the prima donna's idiosyncratic nature, coupled with a genuine understanding of the values held by that individual and emphasis on the attainment of professionally accepted results, will usually inspire the prima donna to shoulder additional responsibility (and perhaps even leadership) in the areas in which he or she is working. Experienced supervisors in this situation usually make every effort to know each person's motivational needs and goals. They study each case to determine the individual's needs in terms of freedom, encouragement, stimulation and self-expression. Only with such understanding will they be able to effectively cope with the prima donna problems that materialize when it comes to the effective delegation of work.

The "one-important-discovery" employee. The problem of the employee who has made one important discovery (but has done nothing well since) is classic. The individual who serendipitously discovers something which "makes the company" can be especially difficult to cope with; he or she feels that "I built this organization with my discovery of the frammis." Some of this type wants to go on making a contribution (indeed, may feel that they have to maintain their reputation) but there are also those who feel that their one important discovery freed them from having to do anything else for the rest of their lives. Delegating work to the latter can be a problem.

Many effective supervisors have found that coping with the "one-important-discovery" type requires first that that individual's talents and capabilities be assessed in the light of his or her past performance—not only by the boss, but also by the boss and the subordinate working together. In this assessment the superior and subordinate should examine, objectively and in detail, any blind spots or points of disagreement. The supervisor should point out how the subordinate's potential can be made more valuable, interpreting it as it relates to the employee's future contribution to the organization. If there are areas in which there are no complaints with the individual's performance, this fact should be spelled out, too, along with the reasons for it. If there are no complaints because the individual's work in that area is good, that's fine. But it could also mean simply that the individual is doing nothing in that area.

Sometimes the subordinate is *unaware* that he or she is regarded as coasting along on the strength of that one important discovery, and is perfectly willing—sometimes even eager—to correct that impression if it is tactfully called to his or her attention by the supervisor.

It should be recognized also that sometimes the "one-important-discovery" employee is labeled as such by competitive and jealous co-workers. Then the supervisor should assess that individual's compatability with his or her co-workers and determine whether he or she has been performing at a satisfactory level (and is likely to continue doing so). If he or she is not insufferable to others and does good work, the problem is in the minds of the individual's co-workers.

The "special-projects-only" addict. Some people who work in highly technical staff or creative work get a feeling that they should work only on certain "special" projects. More often than not, the reason for this attitude is that only certain unique projects may be of interest to them, but they usually are quite good at rationalizing why they should be assigned only to specific projects or certain kinds of work: They have special training or a particular background or certain experience which no one else seems to have. Now, we are not ignoring the fact that some people *do* have very specialized knowledge and experience, but unfortunately, even in highly technological work, assignments to special projects are seldom justified. The reason is, of course, that the (disdained) bread-and-butter work still needs to be done.

Actually it becomes a question of *degree* of structure and control within the total environment in which the work is to be accomplished rather than the right or the wrong way to do it. Practically always good supervisors or managers in highly technological work or specialized staff positions find that teamwork in any work environment—including technical and creative work—*almost always* gets better results than does individual performance. This is not to say that some individuals may not be a good deal more brilliant than perhaps even groups of other people, but the fact has long been established that several individuals working together on a problem almost invariably come up with better ideas than can one individual.

Some people who feel that they are tremendously more qualified (and, therefore, somehow better) than others develop real personnel problems. Most studies have shown that enlightened managements, by establishing conditions which recognize—but never cater to—the needs of the highly technical and professional people working for them (in respect to recognition, self-actualization, achievement, challenging and interesting work, etc.) normally bring about a feeling of camaraderie and involvement within the organization structure. As a result, it is usually unnecessary to use coercive tactics to get any individual to work on one specific project.

A team of high-technology people, working for enlightened management, can usually avoid problems and feelings of indolence, passivity, insubordination, noninvolvement, and emotional disenchantment from the work assigned. This condition usually means that people in management are trying to develop an integrated work environment by developing teamwork in the high-technology, staff, and professional areas. And it can be done.

The "My-interests-are-all-that-is-important" attitude. One of the most debilitating attitudes which people in staff, highly technical, or creative work can assume is that their interests or disciplines are all that is important. Unfortunately, many people devote their attention only to their area of technical expertise, defining anything that is going on in the organization in terms of their areas of responsibility. The personnel specialist who sees psychology as the only source of truth or the physicist who attempts to explain the world only in terms of purely physical phenomena are classic cases of this type. Those not schooled "properly" in these disciplines may not appreciate the tunnel vision of their "betters," and this can cause real disruption in the office or lab. There's nothing wrong with being proud of one's discipline, but each of us must recognize the necessity of integrating our functions effectively with the activities of the rest of the organization.

As in the case of the "special projects only" individual, the boss must fully appreciate the motivational drives and interests of the people who are working for him or her. For high-technology people, at least (and probably for others as well), these include:

- Self esteem, pride in what one is doing and one's personal worth.
- Some degree of autonomy in determining what one is going to do and when one is going to do it.
- The opportunity to express oneself in a wide variety of activities, not only at work but also in such things as art, music, etc.
- A sense of acceptance by and belonging to their work group.
- A degree of security (at least to the extent that one is not threatened from within the organization).

- □ The opportunity for professional growth (which is often closely related to academic and personal growth).

The preceding paragraphs highlight some of the reasons why highly technical and professional people avoid shouldering responsibility. For the most part, technical and staff people are like any other individuals at work: They take pride in what they are doing, and will do as good a job as they possibly can. This is especially true when they feel that they are not being victimized by anyone else's hangups or by deliberately malicious organizational practices or policies. Unfortunately, some individuals are exceptions to this generalization, and coping with these exceptions is the key to effective delegation to staff, technical, and professional people.

Understanding the Staff, Technical, and Professional Point of View

In making work assignments to highly technical or professional people, particularly when it appears that work is not being done as required, or that responsibility has not been shouldered, the supervisor must understand certain ideas if he or she is to be effective. Let us review some of these:

1. To the staff, technical, or professional person, informality is always equated with lack of planning, poor results orientation, and a hit-or-miss attitude toward work. Unfortunately, staff, technical, and professional people practically always have a penchant for scientific rigor, and tend to view any informality as a manifestation of poor planning and a lack of deliberateness or goal orientation on the part of the leader. To cope with this attitude the boss should assume a posture similar to that of a coach. Unfortunately, many people who are in the position of coaching staff, technical, or professional people often don't fully appreciate the rigor they are dealing with, or the results they desire. They want to see accomplished what they have defined as very clear objectives, yet they strongly resist the very rigid attitudes of their subordinates in respect to the quantity and quality of work required, the scheduling of that work, and particularly, the budgetary constraints involved. The boss must word those objectives in a way to which the subordinate can respond effectively.

2. Unless there is any positive reward for taking time to develop one's self *as an employee,* such development will be resisted by the technical or staff employee in deference to his or her professional growth. This does not mean that the highly technical employee *necessarily* will avoid trying to shoulder responsibilities as an employee. However, it must be recognized that the technical or staff specialist's discipline, area of interest, and own personality may be far more important to him or her than are the organization's plans. While the staff specialist can question the validity of this statement, it is generally true.

3. The supervisor must know how to coach, especially in terms of the mind of the subordinate. According to some studies, staff, technical, and professional people feel that there are four essentials of which the boss should be aware:

- ☐ The level of knowledge and creativity required of the employee.
- ☐ The degree of discretion and judgment required of the employee in the effective dispatch of his or her duties.
- ☐ The fact that the intellectual character of the job which the specialist or professional person is doing cannot be reduced to any standardized format.
- ☐ The need to *not be frustrated* at work by having attention deflected toward nonessential functions or duties.

4. The supervisor must know what is required of the individual subordinate to grow professionally and how these requirements fit in with the personal or self-development goals of the individual.

It is one thing to know what is required for success in a particular organizational unit, such as an R and D laboratory or Industrial Relations department. It is something else to be useful to one's subordinate technician or professional individual when one doesn't know what the subordinate's personal or self-development goals are. Staff, technical, or professional people respond best to coaching and/or supervisory-advisory tactics when they can clearly see the usefulness and meaningfulness of such practices to their career development.

Unfortunately, career development is often viewed in an academic and professional light by the highly technical or professional person. The supervisor of such personnel must know what the personal ambitions of his or her people are so that he or she is able to advise subordinates about their career development in terms acceptable to them. This is especially true when coaching or otherwise engaging in personnel development activities with such employees.

Managing technical people is not necessarily different from managing direct supervisors, supervisors of supervisors, or even subordinate managers of managers. The basic psychological dimensions are all there—the boss is bossing the subordinate. The complications arise from the fact that each of them is an individual, so all the foibles of human nature—the breakdowns in communication, the misunderstandings, the pettiness, and other problems—enter into trying to get the job done.

In the staff, technical, or professional area the art and skill of delegation requires not so much that an individual be superhuman or even gifted before he or she can get others to effectively shoulder the responsibility assigned to them. Rather, it requires that performance goals be clearly established and couched in terms meaningful to the subordinate to whom they are being assigned.

CONCLUSION

The *way* work responsibility is assigned varies with the different levels in the organization and according to the kind of work being supervised, but the reader who has read this entire book (rather than just parts of it) will recognize that the behavioral *principles* required for success in delegation are the same at all levels. The rank-and-file worker, the line supervisor, the supervisor of supervisors, and the manager of managers may all give different reasons for refusing to accept work assignments or responsibilities, but their basic motivations for doing so will all be of similar types.

Unfortunately, people expect different things from different individuals, at different levels in the organization; requirements for success as an executive *are* different from the requirements for success as a highly competent technician. Just so, the skills to be mastered by an individual who wants only to be the lead person or foreman in an organization are different from those which must be developed by the person who wants to become a middle-level manager.

Whatever the nature of the individual supervisor's delegation skills, one thing must be made very clear; in plying the fine art and skill of delegation the individual must *know* what his or her own aspirations are in respect to getting results through other people.

EXERCISES

1. As employees, are professional people different from rank and file? How? Are staff people different? How? Explain in detail.
2. What are the problems which you encounter in your job in delegating work to staff, professional, or technical people? How can you overcome these problems?
3. Do you feel that professional, staff, or technical people see different loyalties at work than their loyalty to the company or organization? If so, how? Can anything be done about this? What? Explain in detail.
4. How can you best handle the prima donna at work? What about the "one-big-discovery" person? What about the "I-only-work-on-special-projects" person? What about the "My-area-is-the-only-important-area" person?

INDEX